For 30 years I've smiled inside myse
at the flowery statements of dedica-
tion authors shower upon people. And
now, I silently apologize to each of
them as I dedicate this first book to
my wife Reyhan, and my son Khan.

They have been widow and fatherless
child during the months I have
worked, written, tested and typed
these recipes. Not realizing it, they
were the ones who suffered the hours
of loneliness during the composition
of my book and I love them for it.

I want also to recognize the first
women in my life: Mama, who never
let us go without a good hot meal
prepared with the best and freshest
food available.

Grandma Olivieri and Grandma
Antinore, who, through their modest
efforts, exposed me to the classical
foods from France's southern border
to the Isle of Sicily. Through them I
was privileged to enjoy the color,
culture, cuisine and customs which
are slowly fading from today's world.

And lastly, Marian Russell, my high
school teacher and dear friend, who
so loved food and shared that passion
with me.

You are all reflected in these pages—
thanks!

D1133586

Cooking Good.

Chef Don Antinore

Printed by Cohber Press, Rochester, N.Y. 14623 U.S.A.

Forward

For those of you who have never read Brillat-Savarin's book "The Physiology of Taste," I quote one of the most memorable observations: "Beasts feed, man eats, but the truly perceptive man dines." So, to this end, Chef Don Antinore, American-born and European-bred chef du cuisine, par excellence, has formulated this book. In its presentation, Chef Antinore manages to convey the simple beauties of cooking in a manner which every lay person can share in the culinary secrets of those of us who are committed to the profession of gastronomy.

Chef Antinore's book strongly echoes the intimate style of Chef Edward D'Promaine, who managed to bring each reader into his kitchen and stand at his work table for a personal lesson in the culinary arts. Both chefs delight in relaying to embryonic culinary devotees the ramifications of preparatory measures, the origins of the dish, its sensual and palatal excitements, mental climaxes and residual joys.

As Brillat-Savarin was a sensitive chef in his time, equally so is Chef Antinore today. Chef Antinore does not only prepare food, but he imparts a special panache to every recipe regardless of size, for he imparts also some of his own self to each dish.

Dining properly is important to Chef Antinore; so important that he wants you to share in this experience, that you may realize this in the joys of the table, for these joys mix well with all other pleasures and remain the last to console us.

It is with great pleasure that I, without the slightest hesitation, recommend these pages to all budding gatronomes. Bon Appetit!!

Michael Campbell-Tinney

roduction

oking is as natural to us as eating! It is y belief that because we must eat, ooking must be inherent. We all have the native ability to create sumptuous meals if aware of how to direct that ability. I will call it culinary sense.

I have had several years of fun and thousands of hours of enjoyment in the kitchen. My Chef demonstrated very early that the approach to culinary expression didn't depend so much on a calibrated cup as it did on confidence. I suspected from those early days that the avoidance of pharmaceutical procedure in the kitchen was the best insurance that I would have a good time cooking. It also freed my "cook's soul" to imagine and build magic mountains of gastronomic delights. If I discovered that I was missing an herb or ingredient—instead of panic, I turned the possible disaster around and substituted.

Claude would call across the kitchen to me, "Cooking good, Don Antinore?" and I'd call back, "I don't know, but you'll love it!" And so the title "Cooking Good with Chef Don Antinore" is my tribute to my teacher and culinary guide.

The recipes are mostly classical, although orchestrated All'Antinore. For more than 20 years I have absorbed the methods of sound food preparation and discovered that the long way around was a waste (most of the time). Preparing elegant, tasty dishes easily was more fun and gave me more freedom than wasted hours of measuring and weighing. Sure, some attention has to be given to the proportion of the ingredient to the volume of a recipe—but with practice, it becomes part of our nature.

Included in these pages are recipes which have been proven successful in all modes of kitchens, professional as well as in the home. The procedures are easy, elegant, and the results are guaranteed. You'll find no pretense to their ability to be sound statements.

Acknowledgements

Cover & Title Page Designed by
Wolff Associates, Inc.
Rochester, NY

Cover Photo
Courtesy Gannett Rochester News
Reed Hoffman, Photographer

Title Page Photo
Courtesy Canandaigua Daily Messenger
Diane Zielinsky, Photographer

Proofreader & Recipe Analyst
Millie Mikkanen Baxter
Former Editor & Food Columnist
Rochester Times-Union

Manuscript Typist & Editorial Assistant
Marie DellaPietra

Typography
Rochester Mono/Headliners

Printing
Cohber Press

A special note of gratitude to the many
friends, both professional cooks and
gourmet hobbyists, who tested these recipes.

Thanks to

D. Kirk Doescher, General Manager
and
Rita Ori, Clubhouse Manager,
Food & Beverage Director

of Monroe Golf Club
Pittsford, NY

for their professional support
and considerations during the publication
of this book.

and a special thanks to my Sous Chef,
Gilbert Brien and my culinary staff
for understanding and putting forth the
extra effort needed in the days prior
to publication.

Contents:

*suggests that you refer back to the sauce
  and stock section of this book as you read a
  recipe.

Culinary Terms and Definitions Glossary

So many times while reading recipes, we find ourselves baffled by a term used by the author. Sometimes the book, like this one, includes a glossary—but it's packed away in the back pages. Not so in this book! We hope to make cooking fun and easy and indeed less confusing during the translating of recipes. A practical, usable recipe with easy to understand terms is important to the cook, so I begin with explanations so that you will have a good time cooking as you create from these pages.

Appetizer—Small serving of food which precedes a meal—can be either solid or liquid.

Aspic—A clear jelly usually derived from the sufficient reduction of meat or fish stocks which set or become firm when cooled. Can also apply to stocks to which gelatin is added.

Bake—To cook by means of dry heat, usually in a closed area (oven).

Barbecue—To roast-broil over hot coals or on a revolving frame.

Baste—To moisten by pouring or spooning melted fat, drippings or marinade over roasting food.

Batter—A flour/liquid mixture which can easily be stirred and poured.

Beat—To make any mixture texturally smooth by a regular, brisk circular motion.

Bind—To hold together by mayonnaise or other sauces or to thicken with roux or other agents.

Blanch—To immerse into or pour boiling water over food to pre-cook a little.

Blend—To mix two or more ingredients together so they lose their identity and act as a single agent.

Boil—To cook in liquid which is constantly and rapidly bubbling.

Braise—To cook by searing in hot fat, then simmering in liquid.

Broil—To expose food surfaces to direct high heat, usually from above.

Broth—A liquid in which meat, fish or vegetables have been simmered.

Brown—To darken to a rich golden color thereby sealing in juices.

Canapé—An appetizer made of a small piece of bread (usually toasted) and spread with a seasoned food or paté.

Casserole—A deep dish in which food is cooked and served.

Chop—To cut into irregular pieces.

Compote—Sweetened fruit which has usually been stewed and chilled to keep as whole as possible.

Condiment—Food seasonings: salt, pepper, herbs, spices or prepared mixtures, either sauce, liquid or seasoning.

Crisp-Tender—To cook a vegetable until it's acceptably tender yet retaining some of its original crispness and freshness.

Crush—To smash between two flat surfaces releasing flavors.

Cut—1. To divide food into pieces with a knife or scissors or 2. to incorporate fats into dry ingredients with minimum blending.

Cutlet—A small (thin) slice of meat usually cut from the leg or rib of an animal.

Deglaze—After cooking meat or poultry, pour a little liquid into pan and simmer, scraping up bits of food from the bottom and sides of pan.

Dice—To cut into small uniform cubes.

Dredge—Coat with flour or other dry ingredients.

Dough—A flour/liquid mixture which must be kneaded to blend.

Drippings—Fats and juices resulting from cooking meats.

Entrée—The main part of an informal meal or a subordinate dish served between main courses of a formal meal.

Filet—A portion cut from the center parts of a tenderloin, usually very little fat and no bone.

Fillet—Boneless side of or a whole fish boned.

Fold—To mix or combine foods without losing air bubbles.

Fricassee—To cook by stewing in heavy gravy/sauces.

Fry—To cook in fat or oil.

Fumet—A stock made from fish or meat and reduced with wine until concentrated.

Garnish—To decorate or enhance a plate of food with a bright and savory food substance.

Glaze—To coat a food with a shiny coat.

Grate—To reduce to small particles by rubbing food against a rough surface designed for this purpose (grater).

Julienne—Any food cut into matchstick strips.

Knead—To manipulate with a pressing-folding-stretching motion, usually applied to bread doughs or ground meat mixtures.

Marinade—An oil/acid mixture in which food is allowed to stand to both tenderize and flavor.

Melt—To liquify by heat.

Mignon—Small piece of meat cut from the tenderloin of beef.

Mince—To chop finely.

Mix—To combine by any means which affects distribution and integration.

Parch or Sear—To brown by means of dry high heat, usually in an oven to form a light crust over surface of food.

Pare—To carve away outer covering or skin (apple).

Parboil—To boil raw food only as long as it takes to part cook.

Paté—A paste of ground meat and liver with herbs, spices and fat.

Peel—To strip off the outer coat or rind (orange).

Pureé—A smooth thick sauce-like liquid made by either pressing cooked food through a fine sieve or blended electrically.

Ragout—A thick savory stew in brown sauce.

Reduce—To boil away or steam a liquid to lessen its volume and concentrate its flavors.

Roast—To cook by dry heat, usually in an oven.

Sauté—To cook quickly in very little fat in a shallow fry pan.

Score—To cut lightly or shallow to mark.

Simmer—To cook in a liquid at a temperature below boiling.

Stew—To cook in a small amount of liquid over low heat so as to infuse all flavors and tenderize.

Stir-Fry—An Oriental method of frying in very little and very hot oil which keeps food crisp-tender and appealing.

Stock—A rich extract of meat, fish, poultry or vegetable solubles simmered for a long period of time—bases for soups and sauces.

Toss—The lifting gently of foods or ingredients to blend by a rising-falling action.

Whip—To beat rapidly, increasing volume by the incorporation of air.

Whisk—To stir with a wire utensil to blend and smooth, usually in to sauces.

Zest—The oily rind of citrus fruit grated, to be used as a flavoring.

11

Stocks, Soups & Sauces

Herb Blurb

The eye, nose and mouth are important to the craft of food preparation, and the use of herbs and spices converts that craft into a true art form. It is with herbs and spices that the culinary artist can truly blend bouquet and flavor and create excitement.

The virtual impossibility of detecting the freshness of an herb or spice without sight or smell in your kitchen is evident in the months and even years we keep them around. Dried herbs and spices lose their character and flavor with age and, if allowed to sit on a spice shelf for too long, should be replaced. You know the eating habits as well as the cooking habits in your home, so buy herbs and spices accordingly. If you hardly ever use a seasoning—don't buy a load of it! Buy the least amount possible, or substitute (a good exercise for the more creative cook).

Herbs and spices should enhance the flavor of foods, not overpower them. "More is better" simply doesn't apply to seasonings. "Fresh is best" is a more applicable rule. Whenever possible, use fresh herbs and ground or grated spices as you need them. Pre-ground or dried seasonings may be substituted, but expect to suffer a little. A recipe suggests a dry or ground seasoning, for the convenience of the cook, but if you're able to obtain fresh—"fresh is best!"

Remember, never substitute the same amount of fresh for dried herbs. The dried are essentially more concentrated. If a recipe calls for dry herbs—use more (make double) of fresh.

When doubling a recipe or preparing a recipe for freezing, do not increase the amount of herbs (or spices). Freezing concentrates the flavors and they become more intense with reheating. Adjust to taste—especially the stronger and more aromatic seasonings.

Chef Antinore's Hollandaise Sauce

Yields 2 cups

  1 whole egg
    Juice of 2 lemons
    Dash of tabasco sauce
    Salt
  1 cup clarified butter

Break the egg into a blender container, add the dash of tabasco and salt—blend for 10 seconds. Add the lemon juice and blend 5 seconds. Turn the blender on run and slowly add the butter to the center of whirlpool created in the blender. You'll hear and see the sauce thicken and the whirlpool close. Run ½ minute and turn off. Scrape container clean into a bowl. Serve.

Sauce Béarnaise

Yields 2 cups

  6 tablespoons dry white wine
  6 tablespoons cider vinegar
  2 teaspoons shallots, chopped finely
  ½ teaspoon dry tarragon

In a shallow, small fry pan combine all ingredients and simmer until reduced to almost nothing. Stir into hollandaise sauce. Serve.

Béarnaise Sauce with Tomato "Sauce Choron"

Yields 2 cups

Prepare Sauce Béarnaise and add a half-teaspoon tomato paste and a good pinch of dry chervil. Blend and let set to infuse flavors completely. Serve.

Caper Sauce (For Poached Fish)

Yields 3 cups

Prepare basic butter sauce and at the last moment, add 2-3 tablespoons chopped capers to the sauce. Blend well and serve.

Roux

Roux is the thickening agent used in most classical sauces. The recipe for roux: (to bind 5 cups of stock)

1½ ounces butter
1½ ounces (maybe a slight bit more) flour

Melt the butter in a heavy pan. Add the flour to make a smooth paste. Stir-cook for 2-3 minutes over moderate heat. Roux (paste) should smell like toasted nuts and be nut-brown (golden) in color.

Basic Brown Sauce "Sauce Espagnole"

Yields 4-5 cups

    4 cups basic beef stock
    1 ounce chopped onion
    1 ounce bacon, cooked and cut up
    2 ounces diced carrots
    1 pinch of thyme
    1 bay leaf
    1 ounce cold butter

Sauté onion and bacon until browned—add herbs and carrots. In a heavy saucepan, bring beef stock to boiling point. Stir in roux with wire whisk and blend vigorously until thickened. Add bacon-onion mixture to sauce. Let simmer over lowest heat possible for ½ hour. Add cold butter and blend until melted. Add commercial Kitchen Bouquet to darken to your liking. Strain and serve.

Sauce Demi-Glace

This is the basic brown sauce with 2 tablespoons tomato paste added to the bacon-onion mixture. Cook as directed. Darken with Kitchen Bouquet, strain and serve.

Sauce Mousseline

Yields 2 cups

Prepare 1 recipe of Chef A's Hollandaise sauce to which you add 3 tablespoons freshly whipped sweet cream (heavy) just before serving.

Basic Butter Sauce
Yields 3 cups

1½ ounces butter
1½ cups flour
  2 cups boiling water with a pinch of salt added
  4-5 egg yolks
  2 tablespoons hot milk
  ½ pound soft butter

Melt the butter in a saucepan. Add flour and make a smooth roux. Add the hot water all at once, whisking vigorously until thickened. Lower heat. Beat the hot milk into the egg yolks and stir into the thickened water. Remove from heat and strain. Gradually add the soft butter.

Sauce Cardinal

Basic Béchamel Sauce recipe to which you add and simmer with 6-8 tablespoons heavy cream and 4 ounces lobster butter and a generous dash of cayenne pepper. (Lobster butter can be purchased commercially—saves the work!)

Cream Curry Sauce
Yields 2 cups

  2 ounces butter
  1 tablespoon onion, finely chopped
  1 teaspoon curry powder
1½ cups basic béchamel sauce
  6 tablespoons heavy cream

Melt the butter in a heavy saucepan and sauté onion. As soon as it starts to brown, add curry powder and stir to blend with onion and butter. Add sauce béchamel and whisk to smooth consistency and simmer over lowest possible heat for 10 minutes. Strain and serve.

Oyster Sauce
Serve as needed

Count 3 or 4 whole oysters per person. Warm the oysters in their own juices. Combine the oysters with their juices into 3 tablespoons sauce béchamel made with fish stock.

Simple White Sauce "Velouté"
Yields 4-5 cups

Use a basic chicken stock, 4 cups. Sauté 1 ounce bacon, 1 ounce chopped onion, pinch of thyme, 4 sprigs of parsley, a bay leaf and 1½-2 ounces minced carrots and 1 ounce cold butter.

Bring chicken stock to a boil. Add roux and stir with a wire whisk over moderate heat until thick. Add sauté of bacon, etc. and simmer over lowest possible heat for ½ hour. Add cold butter—stir in. Strain sauce and serve.

Sauce Supreme
Yields 4-5 cups

Prepare a basic white sauce recipe. Add ½ cup condensed chicken stock (which you have reduced to half its original [1 cup] amount by boiling), and stir in 1 cup heavy cream and 4 tablespoons of sherry wine. Mix well with wire whisk. Simmer 10 minutes over lowest heat possible. Strain and serve.

White Wine Sauce "Béchamel"
Yields 4-5 cups

    4 cups whole milk
       A pinch of salt and freshly milled white
       pepper
       A dash ground nutmeg
    1 clove
       A thick slice of fresh onion
       A sprig of fresh parsley
    1 bay leaf, whole
       A pinch of thyme
    ¼ cup dry white wine at room temperature
       Cold butter

In a heavy saucepan, combine milk, onion, herbs and spices and bring to the boiling point (don't scald milk!)—reduce heat to low. Simmer for 15 minutes. Add roux and stir with a wire whisk until thickened. Add wine slowly (whisking throughout addition of wine) and simmer 5 minutes over lowest heat possible. Blend in cold butter. Strain and serve.

Sauce Mornay
Yields 2 cups

Warm 1½ cups sauce béchamel over low heat. With the first sign of boiling, whisk smooth with wire whisk. At the last moment, add 3 ounces cold butter and 4 tablespoons grated good Parmesan cheese. Keep stirring. Smooth and infuse all ingredients. Serve.

Hunter's Sauce "Sauce Chasseur"
Yields 3 cups

1½ cups mushroom sauce
  1 teaspoon butter
  1 teaspoon chopped onion with a bit of garlic (or 1 teaspoon shallots)
  3 tablespoons brandy
  6-8 tablespoons dry white wine
  2-3 sprigs parsley
  1 ounce cold butter

In a heavy saucepan, sauté the shallots (onions) in butter until browned a little. Add the brandy and white wine and simmer 5 minutes. Add the sauce demi-glace and whisk thoroughly to blend. Simmer for 10 minutes over lowest possible heat. Finish with butter, strain and serve.

Basic Tomato Sauce
  1 clove fresh garlic, peeled and cut up
  2 tablespoons olive oil
  3 pounds ripe tomatoes or 6 cups canned plum tomatoes
    Pinch of salt and freshly milled pepper
  1 tablespoon dry or fresh sweet basil

In a heavy skillet, sauté the garlic in the olive oil until toasty brown and remove. Add all the tomatoes with the seasonings and basil and simmer in open pan for 20 to 30 minutes. Sieve and cool. Use as recipe directs.

Mushroom Sauce "Sauce Champignon"
Yields 5 cups

Prepare a basic Sauce Demi-Glace. Sauté 1 cup sliced fresh mushrooms in a little butter. Add ¼ cup cream sherry wine to sauté and simmer 3-5 minutes. Add the mushroom-wine mixture to simmering sauce. Adjust seasonings (salt and freshly milled pepper).

Sauce Bordelaise (Bordeaux)
Yields 2 cups

1½ cups basic sauce demi-glace
  ¼ cup dry red Bordeaux wine
  1 teaspoon shallots, chopped (substitute a little onion and garlic, minced)
    Salt and freshly milled pepper to taste
  1 ounce cold butter

In a saucepan, combine wine and chopped shallots (onion-garlic minced) and simmer for 5 minutes over high heat. Add the sauce demi-glace and stir in with a wire whisk until flavors completely infuse. Season with salt and fresh pepper—add butter. Strain and serve.

Sauce Bourguignonne (Burgundy)
Yields 2 cups

1½ cups sauce demi-glace
  1 ounce butter
  2 ounces fatty bacon
  2 tablespoons chopped onion
  2 tablespoons chopped carrot
  1 bay leaf
    Pinch of thyme
    Sprig of parsley
    Dry Burgundy wine
  1 ounce cold butter

In a heavy saucepan, melt the butter and sauté chopped bacon, onion and carrot and brown lightly. Add the herbs and Burgundy wine. Boil until reduced by half its original volume. Add the sauce demi-glace and whisk in to blend. Adjust seasonings (salt and fresh pepper). Finish with cold butter. Strain and serve.

Artichoke Sauce All'Antinore (Serve on Fettucine)

Serves 6-8

½ cup olive oil (no substitutes)
2 medium onions, peeled and chopped fine
3 (or more) cloves garlic, peeled, crushed and minced
2 cans of artichoke hearts. Quarter the hearts and reserve the liquid for later.
1 pound fresh white mushrooms, washed and sliced
1 heaping teaspoon fresh sweet basil (or ½ teaspoon dry)
1 teaspoon chopped fresh parsley (or ½ teaspoon dry)
Crushed red pepper to your taste (hot)
Salt and freshly ground pepper to taste
4-5 tablespoons grated Romano cheese (no substitutes)

In a large skillet heat oil and sauté garlic and onion until tender. Add quartered artichoke hearts and mushrooms and continue to sauté until mushrooms are tender. Add sweet basil, parsley, red pepper and salt and pepper to taste and stir to mix. Simmer for 2-3 minutes or until you enjoy a pleasant aroma of this mixture. Finally add reserved liquid from artichokes and simmer for 8-10 minutes

Into boiling water add a few drops of oil and cook the Fettucine to the degree of doneness which suits your taste. Drain well and run hot water over pasta to wash off any excess starch. Place washed pasta onto a warm platter and pour the freshly created sauce on top. Sprinkle Romano cheese over pasta and sauce, serve.

Suggested Wine: A semi-dry Italian white— perfect for this splendid appointment.

Fish Stock

2 pounds of fresh fish with heads and bones, cut up
1 medium onion, cut into quarters
Dash salt
1 cup dry white wine
Few sprigs of fresh parsley
1 bay leaf
Pinch of thyme
Leaves from 3 celery stalks
10 peppercorns
Water

Fish Stock (continued)

Place fish, onion, salt, wine, herbs, celery, and peppercorns into a 3-quart sauce pan. Cover with water and simmer for 2 hours. Cool and strain. Add a little lemon juice if you like. If more concentrated flavor is desired, "reduce" over high heat.

Beef Stock

    1 pound lean beef cubes
    1 pound lean veal cubes
    ½ pound beef bones
    3 carrots, cut into thirds
    1 tomato, quartered
    2 medium onions, quartered with skin on
    3 stalks of celery, broken in half, leaf and all
    2 cloves of garlic, peeled
      A bay leaf
      A pinch of dry thyme or a sprig of fresh thyme if you have one
      A few sprigs of fresh parsley
      Water

Place meats, vegetables and herbs into an 8-quart heavy pot (Dutch oven is best) and add enough water to half fill the pot and simmer open for about 2½ hours. Cool and strain. If you desire a more concentrated flavor, "reduce" the stock further.

Chicken Stock

    5 pounds chicken backs and wings or a stewing chicken (fowl)
    3 fresh carrots cut into thirds
    2 medium onions, quartered with skin on
    3 stalks of celery broken in half with leaves
      Salt
      A pinch each of thyme and rosemary
      A bay leaf
      A few sprigs of fresh parsley
    2 whole cloves
      Water

Place chicken, vegetables, herbs and spices into an 8-quart pot (Dutch oven is best) and cover with water (3½ to 4 quarts) and simmer open for 2½ to 3 hours. Cool and strain. You will probably want to remove the fat—best to do after refrigeration and set hard. If you desire a more concentrated stock, "reduce" further over high heat.

Cream of Chicken and Curry Soup

Serves 6

   3 cups of chicken stock*
   1 small carrot, peeled and diced small
   1 small onion, peeled and chopped finely
   2 celery stalks, strings removed and diced
     small
     Salt and freshly milled pepper to taste
   ¼ teaspoon marjoram
   2 teaspoon curry powder
   ¼ teaspoon crushed peppercorns
   1 cup Half and Half at room temperature
   1 cup diced cooked chicken
   ⅓ cup cooked rice
     Chopped chives

In a heavy pot cook celery, onion and carrot in stock for 10-15 minutes or until tender. Add all seasonings, chicken meat and rice and simmer 10 minutes more. Stir in cream, heat through and serve. Garnish each serving with chopped chives.

Garlic Soup

Serves 6

6-8 cloves fresh garlic, peeled and crushed
   6 tablespoons olive oil
     Dash cayenne pepper
   6 slices of white bread, crusts removed and
     cubed
   6 cups chicken stock*
     Pinch of salt
   2 tablespoons chopped fresh parsley
   4 eggs beaten

In a heavy, large saucepan, sauté garlic in the olive oil and cayenne until pale gold. Remove garlic with slotted spoon and reserve. Fry bread cubes in the same oil until toast brown. Pour in chicken stock, garlic and a pinch of salt. Cover and simmer for a half hour. Blend in beaten eggs slowly, stirring constantly and cook 5 minutes until lightly thickened. Garnish each serving with fresh parsley.

Lobster Bisque
Serves 6

  2 tablespoons butter
  1 tablespoon fresh onion, peeled and minced
  2 tablespoons flour
  1 tablespoon tomato paste
  2 cups chicken stock (reduced from 3 cups)*
1½ cups cooked lobster meat, cut up small
  ¼ cup dry white wine at room temperature
  2 cups Half and Half at room temperature
    A pinch of salt
    Dash cayenne pepper

Sauté minced onion in butter until soft, using a heavy large sauce pan. Add flour and tomato paste and stir until completely blended into a roux. Add hot reduced chicken stock and whisk until slightly thickened. Stirring, add wine and cream and allow bisque to thicken again. Add lobster and heat through. Season with salt and cayenne just before serving.

Shrimp Bisque
Serves 6

  1 pound small (not tiny) shrimp, cooked, peeled and deveined (reserve 1 cup stock)
  2 tablespoons minced fresh celery
  2 green onions, minced from end to end
  ¼ cup melted butter
  2 tablespoons flour
    Generous pinch paprika
    Dash of freshly milled pepper
  2 cups of milk at room temperature
  1 cup chicken stock (reduced from 2 cups)*
  1 cup shrimp stock

Coarsely chop shrimp. In a deep, large, heavy saucepan, sauté celery and green onion in butter until tender. Blend in flour and season to make a roux. Add milk and both chicken and shrimp stock and whisk until thickened. Add shrimp and simmer 10 minutes over very low heat. Dot the top of each cup or bowl of bisque with a piece of cold butter, sprinkle with paprika and pepper and serve.

Fish, Seafood & Shellfish

Something's Fishy

If one were to set out to learn all there was to know about fish cookery, he would have to resign himself to the fact that there are more branches to it than schools in the sea. One thing to learn is that a fish is fresh only when its eyes are bulging and arrogantly bright, when its flesh is elastic and your fingers leave no impression after you press it to check it, when its scales are tight to the body and the smell of it is sweet and clean. At the slightest variance of one or any of these—don't buy!

Anoint all fish, seafood and shellfish with lemon juice—they have an affinity for one another.

If you're a lobster lover, and I don't know many who aren't, here are a few tips. Live lobster fans usually live in the "inland" areas of the world, so it's good to know that North Atlantic lobsters will stay alive for about 2 weeks outside their natural habitat—provided they're kept moist with ice or seaweed and water. If you have any doubt about the condition of a live lobster, simply pick it up (or have the dealer do it for you) and observe its tail movement. If it is limp or barely shows signs of movement—the beast is in for an early demise (if not gone already). However, if the tail snaps underneath, you have a lively thoroughbred destined to be firm and luscious.

The best way to boil lobster is not to boil them—steam them. When buying precooked lobster, check the tail and again—if its loose and limp, the lobster was probably dead or nearly so at the time it was cooked. The tail must be curled under and tight to its underside to have been good, alive and fresh.

Shrimp can only be as fresh as possible if you stand aboard a shrimp boat. Otherwise, they are beheaded and frozen as soon after they're caught as possible to insure the original flavor will be kept intact.

Salmon Fillet Steaks And Sauce All'Antinore

Serves 4

- 4 salmon steaks from the fillet
  Salt and freshly milled pepper to taste
  Cayenne pepper
- 2 tablespoons chopped chives
- 2 tablespoons chopped fresh parsley
- ½ pound butter to be used throughout recipe
- 6 ounces mushrooms
- 2 egg yolks
- 3 ounces bread crumbs
  White wine
  Juice of 2 lemons
- 5 ounces Gruyere cheese, grated
  Paprika to garnish

SAUCE:

- 4 tablespoons butter
- 3 tablespoons scallions, finely chopped
- 1 teaspoon mild French mustard
- 2 teaspoons chopped parsley
- 2 teaspoons tomato paste
- 3 tablespoons white vinegar
  A good pinch of tarragon
  Salt and freshly ground pepper
  White wine
- 2 cloves of crushed garlic

SAUCE ALL'ANTINORE:

Heat the butter gently in a saucepan adding scallions, mustard, tomato paste, parsley, tarragon, vinegar, salt, pepper, and wine. Cook all this for a couple minutes. Then add garlic and simmer another 2-3 minutes.

Preheat oven to 500°. Be sure the fillet steaks are dry and sprinkle with salt, cayenne pepper, chives and chopped parsley and finally dribble some butter over all. Place steaks on a well buttered ovenproof dish and pour the sauce All'Antinore over all. Place in the preheated oven (500°) for about 10 minutes or until fish is very firm to the pressure touch of your fingertips. Place just enough butter in the bottom of a frypan to cover and add sliced mushrooms with the juice of ½ a lemon, a dash of salt and pepper to taste. Sauté gently for 3 minutes.

Salmon Fillet Steaks (continued)

Remove the fillet steaks from the oven and keep warm on a platter. Strain the drippings from the oven pan into a stainless bowl and cool a little . . . then add the egg yolks and with a wire whisk beat well. Set aside just long enough to set a saucepan on the stove over high heat to act as heat source for last steps in making the sauce. Place the egg yolk mixture over the boiling water and add the remaining Sauce All'Antinore to the bowl. Stir over the heat until thickened. Add the sautéed mushrooms to the sauce and remove from heat.

Mix the bread crumbs with the remaining lemon juice, wine, and grated cheese. Spoon some of the Sauce All'Antinore over the steaks, sprinkle lavishly with bread crumb mixture and place under the broiler until browned nicely and crisp. Replace to platter and serve with remaining sauce to pass.

Suggested Wine: Meursault '69! Rich and savory but smooth and mellow—a Côte de Beaune wine

Brook Trout Sauté Meuniere
Serves 4

   4 whole filleted brook trout
     Milk, enough to half fill a shallow bowl
   ¼ cup all purpose flour
     Pinch of salt and freshly milled pepper to taste
   ¼ cup cooking oil
   ¼ cup melted butter
  12 lemon slices
     Fresh parsley, chopped

Mix the flour with salt and pepper. Dip each trout in milk bath, then dredge through seasoned flour to coat. Heat the ¼ cup of cooking oil in a heavy skillet and sauté trout until golden brown on both sides. Remove to a warm platter. Pour melted butter over, dust with chopped fresh parsley and garnish with 3 lemon slices each.

Suggested Wine: Chateau Meillant, as young as possible.

Salmon Louise

Serves 4

4 salmon steaks
⅔ cup white wine
Juice of 1 lemon
1 small onion, quartered
6 peppercorns
Watercress sprigs to garnish

TOMATO SAUCE LOUISE
1 bunch green onions, shredded
2 tablespoons butter
½ cucumber, peeled, cut into coarse
matchsticks, blanched and drained
½ pound tomatoes, skinned and quartered
Salt and freshly milled pepper to taste
Chopped parsley

Poach the steaks in the wine with lemon juice, onion and peppercorns added, in a covered dish in a moderate oven (350°) for about 15 minutes, depending on the thickness of the fish, until just cooked. Carefully remove the skin from the salmon.

Meanwhile, prepare the sauce. Sauté the green onions in melted butter. Add the cucumber sticks and sauté quickly. Stir in the tomatoes and heat through carefully. Season, adding a little parsley.

Spoon the tomato sauce into a dish and place salmon on top. Spoon on tarragon-flavored mayonnaise and watercress.

Suggested Wine: Cheverny—a light, but sharp Toine country wine.

Baked Florida Red Snapper

Serves 4

4 8-ounce frozen (or fresh) red snapper fillets
½ cup frozen orange juice, concentrate
¼ pound butter, melted
1 tablespoon soy sauce
Salt and freshly milled pepper to taste
Lemon wedges and chopped parsley

Thaw frozen fillets. Combine orange juice, butter, soy sauce, salt and pepper and mix thoroughly. Place snapper fillets in shallow baking dish, brush with orange mixture and bake in 400° oven for 15-18 minutes, or until fish flakes easily with fork. Baste twice during baking. Remove to warm platter and serve garnished with lemon wedges and chopped parsley.

Broiled Trout Mario
Serves 4

½ cup butter
2 cloves minced fresh garlic
12 raw shrimp, peeled and deveined
¾ cup raw oysters
A cup fresh mushrooms, sliced
A pinch of Spanish saffron (optional)
1 pound can of whole peeled tomatoes
1 cup fish stock*
Generous dash cayenne pepper
Salt and freshly milled pepper to taste
2 tablespoons cornstarch—¼ cup water
2 8-ounce trout, filleted
Dry white wine

Melt butter in a heavy skillet and sauté garlic, shrimp and oysters until shrimp has lost its transparent appearance (5 minutes). Add mushrooms and saffron and stir-fry 2 minutes longer. Add tomatoes (crushing gently with your hands as you add them), fish stock, cayenne, salt and fresh pepper. Simmer 15 minutes. Combine cornstarch with water and add—stirring until sauce thickens. Remove from heat. Broil trout until golden brown and remove to a warm platter. Smother fish with shrimp-oyster sauce and serve.

Suggested Wine: A crisp chilled California Chablis wine.

Crispy Baked Haddock
Serves 4

4 8-ounce haddock fillets
Salt and freshly milled pepper
½ cup evaporated milk
1 cup cornflakes, crushed rather finely
1 egg beaten into evaporated milk

Mix salt and pepper with cornflakes. Dip each haddock fillet into evaporated milk mixture, then into cornflakes. Place in shallow baking dish and bake in 425° oven for 20-25 minutes. Remove to lettuce-lined platter and garnish with radish rosettes and lemon wedges.

Suggested Wine: Vouvray, sparkling white—nicely chilled

Red Snapper à la Yucatan
Serves 4

- ½ cup fresh onion, peeled and chopped
- 3 tablespoons olive oil
- ¾ cup Spanish "stuffed" olives, chopped
- ½ cup mixed red and green sweet bell peppers, chopped
- 2 teaspoons ground coriander
- ½ cup fresh lemon juice
- ½ cup fresh orange juice
  Salt and freshly milled pepper to taste
- 2 red snapper fillets, cut in half (6 ounces each piece)
  Garnish of chopped hard boiled eggs, sliced red radishes, sliced green onion, from end to end and, shredded iceberg lettuce

Heat oil in a heavy large skillet and sauté onions until soft. Add chopped olives and bell peppers and stir-fry 5 minutes over high heat. Lower heat to moderate setting, add lemon and orange juice and season with salt and fresh pepper and coriander. Place red snapper pieces into a buttered shallow ovenproof dish, large enough to hold without crowding. Reduce sauce 5 minutes—pour over fish and bake uncovered at 400° for 30 minutes. Remove carefully to a warm platter. Spoon sauce over and garnish around edged dish with sliced and shredded vegetables. Serve.

Suggested Wine: A dry, lively Sauvignon Blanc (California).

Sea Scallops Sauté with Sherry and Bacon
Serves 4

- 1½ pounds fresh sea scallops
- ½ pound bacon, cut into 1 inch pieces and cooked—reserve fat
- 4 tablespoons butter
  Flour
  Salt and freshly milled pepper
- 1 clove fresh garlic, peeled and minced
  Sherry wine

Lightly flour the scallops. Heat butter and bacon fat in a heavy skillet and add garlic and scallops, sauté until browned. Add cooked bacon pieces and stir. Adjust seasonings to taste and add sherry wine. Simmer for 5 minutes more and serve.

Suggested Wine: Sherry Fino!

Fillet of Sole in Vermouth

Serves 4

- 8 fillets of sole
- 6 ounces dry vermouth
  Salt and freshly milled pepper to taste
  Finely chopped parsley
- ¾ cup fish stock
- 3 cups cold water
- ½ cup white wine
- 1 medium onion
- 1 medium carrot
- 1 medium leek
- ½ pint heavy cream at room temperature
- 4 egg yolks

To **cold** water add white wine, carrot, onion, and leek. Simmer over low heat for about 30 minutes. Strain and discard vegetables. Season stock and allow it to reduce to half its volume. Lay fillets of sole in the palm of your hand and carefully fold both ends to the center. Then fold again (this makes for easier handling and is more attractive when done). Place fillets carefully into the deep skillet around the outside, then the center. Cover the sole with about 3 ounces of vermouth and fish stock. Cover the pan and poach the fish gently over a low heat for about 10 minutes. Drain off most of the stock from poached fillets. Bring stock to a boil. Sprinkle fish with a little vermouth, lower heat and season. Simmer a moment. Set aside. Strain boiling stock once again through a very fine sieve. Place in a clean pan and continue to reduce over high heat. Mix about ½ cup stock and the ½ pint of heavy cream. Bring to a boil. Place fillets of sole onto a warm serving platter. Beat egg yolks in a bowl and beat cream sauce into yolks. Pour back into pan and stir sauce together over low heat until thick. DO NOT BOIL or you will curdle eggs and ruin the delicate sauce. Coat the fillets with the sauce and arrange on an ovenproof platter or baking dish. Place under a hot broiler for a few moments to bubble and slightly color. Serve with lemon wedges.

Suggested Wine: Seyssel—a delicate dry white from Savoie

Baked Fresh Lake Whitefish with Almond and Herb Stuffing

Serves 6-8

1½ sticks butter
1 medium onion, peeled and chopped
2 cups fine bread crumbs
½ cup celery finely chopped
½ cup green pepper, chopped finely
2 cloves of garlic, crushed and minced
2 tablespoons chopped fresh parsley
3 slightly beaten eggs
Salt and freshly milled black pepper
1 teaspoon dried tarragon (2 teaspoons fresh)
½-⅔ cup toasted almonds, coarsely chopped
1 7-pound whitefish, sealed and butterflied with head on
1 cup white dry wine

Preheat the oven to 400°.

In a heavy skillet, melt 2-3 tablespoons butter and sauté onion and garlic until onion is soft but not browned. Add bread crumbs, celery, green pepper, parsley, eggs, season with salt and freshly milled pepper, tarragon and almonds. Mix well and stuff the fish (to stuff fish, lay on its side and open like a book; place stuffing on bottom portion and fold top portion over to cover dressing). Melt remaining butter—line a casserole or baking dish large enough to hold fish comfortably with foil. Place fish and pour wine over—baste with a little of the melted butter and dust with additional milled black pepper.

Place fish uncovered into the 400° oven and bake for 1 hour, basting with butter and wine often. Fish is done when it feels very firm to the pressure of your fingertips or until it flakes easily with a fork. Carefully remove to a platter to serve. Garnish with lemon wedges and fresh parsley sprigs.

Suggested Wine: Gold Seal—Chas. Fournier Champagne.

Pike Milanese with Raisin Sauce
Serves 4

    3 pounds of pike fillets (4 pieces)
    3 cups dry white wine
    1 large carrot, peeled and diced
    1 tablespoon fresh parsley, minced
    2 bay leaves
    1 medium onion, peeled and diced
    Dash of salt
    1 cup seedless raisins
    1 tablespoon butter

Place pike fillets, carrot, onions, bay leaves, parsley and salt into a wide mouth pan—add wine and simmer 30 minutes. Remove fish to a warm platter. Add raisins and simmer an additional 15 minutes to reduce liquid. Add butter and "plumped up" raisins. Remove bay leaves and discard. Pour some of the sauce over fish. Remove vegetables with a slotted spoon and use as garnish. Serve hot.

Suggested Wine: Soavé, chilled and refreshingly young.

Mackerel à la Marinara
Serves 4

    ½ pound spaghetti, cooked al denté
    2 tablespoons olive oil
    1 small onion, peeled and sliced
    1 clove garlic, peeled and crushed
    Pinch each of sweet basil and oregano
    1 tablespoon chopped fresh parsley
    1 small can peeled tomatoes, drained and juice
    reserved
    2 tablespoons reserved tomato juice
    Salt and freshly milled pepper to taste
    4 pieces mackerel (3 pounds) fillets
    Grated Romano cheese

Heat the olive oil in a heavy deep skillet and sauté onions and garlic until browned. Add tomatoes (crushing in your hand), tomato juice, sweet basil, oregano, salt and fresh pepper—cook for 10 minutes. Add mackerel fillets and simmer covered for 10 minutes longer. Place cooked spaghetti on a warm platter and place the four fish pieces on top and spoon marinara sauce over all. Dust with grated Romano cheese and parsley before serving.

Suggested Wine: Chianti Classico, a light red wine with all the gusto of Italy in its character.

Baked Halibut Steak in Sour Cream and Basil Sauce

Serves 4

4 8-ounce halibut steaks (thaw if frozen)
½ cup flour
  Salt and freshly milled pepper
1 teaspoon paprika
  Dash of cayenne pepper
1 or 2 cloves fresh garlic, peeled, crushed and minced
1 medium onion—peeled, halved and sliced thick
¼ cup butter
½ tablespoon chopped fresh sweet basil or 1 teaspoon dry
1 cup sour cream
½ cup dry white wine
  Chopped parsley for garnish

Season the flour with salt and fresh pepper, cayenne, and paprika and lightly coat halibut steaks.

Melt butter in a large heavy skillet and sauté the garlic and onion slices for 2 minutes; push aside and add halibut steaks. Brown the fish and carefully turn, browning the other side. Spoon the garlic-onion mixture over the fish steaks and add the sweet basil, sour cream and wine. Cover and simmer for 5-6 minutes. Shake the pan back and forth to help the sauce thicken. Remove to a heated platter and dust with parsley, then serve.

Suggested Wine: A refreshing German Mosel.

Shrimp de Jonghe All'Antinore

Serves 4

Cook 2 pounds of fresh shrimp which you have cleaned, shelled and deveined. A little under done best.

Combine the following in a blender container:

½ cup melted whole butter
¼ cup dry white wine
½ cup finely chopped parsley leaf and stems
4 cloves fresh garlic, crushed and minced very finely
½ teaspoon Hungarian paprika
  A good dash of cayenne pepper
  Salt and freshly milled pepper to taste
  Juice of 2 lemons

Shrimp de Jonghe (continued)

Turn machine to blend and create a smooth paste with 1½-2 cups of fine bread crumbs (paste wants to be firm, but moist and not hard to fingertip touch).

Place enough of the parsley-garlic paste on the bottom of 9" by 9" shallow baking dish and place shrimp on top. Spread remaining paste over shrimp and bake in 400 degree oven 15-18 minutes or until paste browns a little. Serve with lemon wedges.

All'Antinore Deep Sea Scallops with Braised Lettuce
Serves 4

1½ pounds fresh scallops
  1 cup shredded iceberg lettuce
  1 clove of fresh garlic, peeled and minced
  3 green onions, minced finely
    Flour
    Sherry wine
    Salt and freshly milled pepper
  6 tablespoons butter

Lightly flour the scallops. Melt the butter in a heavy skillet and sauté the scallops with the garlic until lightly browned. Add the minced green onion and the shredded lettuce and gently stir until lettuce has wilted and the onions give off a soft bouquet. Season with salt and fresh pepper, add sherry wine and simmer for 2 minutes. Serve.

Suggested Wine: Muscadet—a delicious dry white from Brittany.

Salt Codfish and Herb Casserole
Serves 6-8

  2 pounds salt codfish
  6 potatoes peeled, blanched and sliced
  1 cup olive oil (vegetable will substitute)
  6 medium onions, peeled, halved and sliced
  4 (or more) cloves garlic, peeled and crushed
  ½ teaspoon thyme
  ½ teaspoon cumin seed
  ½ cup chopped fresh parsley
    Freshly milled pepper to taste
  1 bay leaf
  1 cup dry white wine
  1 cup tomato juice
  ¼ teaspoon tabasco sauce
  ½ cup bread crumbs
  ½ cup grated cheese

Salt Codfish (continued)

Soak the codfish overnight in cold water—drain and rinse thoroughly in fresh cold water, then drain again. Cut fish into 2-inch pieces. Blanch the potatoes—cool slightly and slice into rather heavy pieces.

Heat the oil in a deep, heavy kettle and sauté onions and garlic until soft. Add herbs and spices (pepper, thyme, bay leaf, cumin and parsley), and stir well. Allow seasonings to simmer for a minute or so—then add tomato juice, wine and tabasco. Continue to simmer for 5 minutes (allowing this mixture to fully integrate). Add fish and potato slices and cook until potato is tender (10-15 minutes). Place all into a shallow baking dish, sprinkle with bread crumbs and grated cheese and bake for approximately 10 minutes at 400°—or until golden.

Champagne Poached Fillet of Sole

Serves 4

    1 pound fresh asparagus spears (frozen will
       sub, thawed)
     *A light court bouillon for fish
    8 small fillets of sole (2 each person)
    2 cups cooked and clean shrimp
2-3 ounces gouda cheese, shredded
    1 cup champagne
*½ cup Chef A's hollandaise sauce

In a heavy deep skillet: Simmer clean asparagus in the court bouillon for 3-4 minutes. If fresh, remove and set aside. Lay the fish fillets on a flat surface. Pureé the shrimp in your blender or food processor. Remove from blender, spread some shrimp paté on the sole fillets and place 2 asparagus spears. Divide cheese evenly over fillets. Roll the sole around the asparagus, cheese and shrimp and place in the simmering stock, seam side down. Poach for about 5-8 minutes or until the fish feels firm to the pressure of the back of a fork or your fingertips. Pour in the champagne and let the fish sit in the stock an additional 5 minutes. Remove fillets of sole with a slotted spoon (be careful, they'll break easily if you're not!) and place on a heated platter. Spoon hollandaise over each roll, garnish with lemon wedges and serve.

Suggested Wine: Cold champagne!

Broiled Bay Scallops and Spiced Peaches
Serves 6

    1 pound fresh tiny bay scallops
    2 tablespoons butter
    2 tablespoons lemon juice
      Salt and freshly milled pepper to taste
    6 fresh ripe peaches, peeled, halved and stone
      removed (or 12 canned peach halves)
    ¼ teaspoon each: ground cinnamon, ground
      clove, and mace
    3 slices of raw bacon

Melt butter and combine scallops, lemon juice, salt and fresh pepper and let it sit 15 minutes. Meanwhile, place peach halves in a baking dish (hollow side up). Mix the spices together and sprinkle over peach halves—with a little sprinkle of salt. Spoon the scallops and marinade onto the peaches evenly distributed. Cut bacon into quarters and place a piece on each stuffed peach half. Broil about 4 inches from heat for 8-10 minutes or until bacon is crisp. Serve from the casserole at the table.

Suggested Wine: any good dry New York State white.

Codfish à la Portugaise
Serves 4

    2 pounds of fresh cod or fresh scrod fillets
    2 medium onions, peeled and sliced thinly
  2-3 sweet red peppers, halved, seeded and sliced
      thinly
      Olive oil
      Salt and freshly milled pepper to taste
    4 medium ripe tomatoes, cut into eights
    3 tablespoons fresh parsley, chopped
    1 bay leaf
    6 tablespoons dry white wine or dry sherry

Heat olive oil in a heavy skillet (with cover) and fry sliced onions and red peppers until soft (not browned). Add fish fillets, season with salt and fresh pepper to taste. Add tomato wedges, bay leaf and chopped parsley. Cover and cook 15 minutes over medium heat. Remove to a shallow platter and spoon natural vegetable sauce over fish. Serve.

Suggested Wine: A young California red—a Burgundy style dry wine.

Salmon Mousse All'Antinore

Yield: 2-quart mold

  2 tablespoons unflavored gelatin
1½ cups cold fish stock* (or cold poach
     water—see below)
  ½ cup mayonnaise
     Juice of ½ lemon
  1 pound salmon fillet—poached in *Court
     Bouillon
  1 tablespoon Madeira wine (cream sherry,
     substitute)
     Salt and freshly milled pepper to taste
  ½ cup heavy cream, whipped
     Thin lemon and cucumber slices for garnish

Sprinkle gelatin over cold stock, then heat to dissolve completely. Stirring with a wire whisk, blend in mayonnaise and lemon juice and allow to cool until slightly thickened. Meanwhile, mash salmon coarsely with Madeira wine in an electric blender. Fold salmon-wine mixture into the thickened gelatin gently. Add seasonings (salt and fresh pepper) to taste. Fold in whipped cream and pour into a 2-quart mold. Chill until set. Unmold and surround with lemon and cucumber slices. Serve.

Stuffed Shrimp Charles A.

Serves 4

  8 extra large shrimp (under 10 count), shelled
     and deveined
  3 oz. butter
  1 small onion, peeled and minced finely
  1 clove garlic, peeled, crushed and minced
     finely
  1 small can chopped clams, drained
  6 ounces crabmeat, chopped
  8 saltine crackers, crushed into fine crumbs
  ½ pint heavy cream

Preheat oven to 400°.

Stuffing: Sauté the onion and garlic in a heavy skillet until lightly browned. Add clams and crabmeat and heat through. Sprinkle in cracker crumbs and stir in cream.

Cut a pocket in the back of each shrimp (careful not to cut through). Stuff with stuffing mixture. Place on a broiler pan and bake for 10-12 minutes.

Suggested Wine: Pouilly-Fuissé, 1974.

Deep Sea Scallops in Ginger Sauce

Serves 4

    2 cups fish stock*
    1 tablespoon minced fresh ginger root
    3 tablespoons dry sherry wine
    ½ teaspoon ground ginger
    1 to 1½ pounds deep sea scallops
    ¾ cup chopped fresh celery
    2 teaspoons arrowroot (or cornstarch)
      Cold water
      Salt
      Chopped fresh parsley for garnish

Combine stock and fresh ginger root and simmer until reduced to one cup stock, strain and return to a heavy skillet. Add the sherry and ground ginger along with the scallops and celery and cook until the scallops are tender. Remove scallops to small shell dishes (if you have them) or to a nice but warm platter. Mix arrowroot with a little cold water and stir into the stock and keep stirring until sauce thickens. Taste it, adjust seasoning with salt and spoon over scallops, sprinkle with parsley and serve.

Suggested Wine: A Marino, Italian dry white wine—a lot of character.

Shrimp with Lemon

Serves 4

    24 jumbo shrimp
     8 teaspoons olive oil
     4 tablespoons sweet onion, chopped
     4 teaspoons chopped parsley
     4 cloves garlic
     4 slices lemon
     4 thin slices ham (boiled)
    ¾ cup dry white wine
     4 tablespoons butter

Devein and clean raw shrimp and sauté in olive oil for 5 minutes or until the shrimp turn white and curl. Add onion, garlic, parsley, ham, lemon and butter. Lower heat and simmer 5 minutes. Add the dry white wine and allow to simmer an additional 2 minutes. Garnish with more lemon slices and parsley.

Suggested Wine: An alive wine from the north of Italy—Asti region.

Ocean Perch Espagnole
Serves 4

  4-8 ounces ocean perch fillets
  8 tablespoons melted butter
    Flour
  ½ cup onion, chopped finely
  2 cups canned whole tomatoes
  ¼ cup green pepper, chopped
  1 clove garlic, crushed and chopped finely
  ½ teaspoon sugar
    Salt and freshly milled pepper
  1 bay leaf
  2 whole cloves
  1 cup sliced fresh mushrooms

Melt butter in a heavy skillet and sauté onion and garlic until tender. Add remaining ingredients (except fillets and flour) and cook for 10-15 minutes. Dredge fillets through flour and place in a greased shallow baking dish. Cover with Spanish sauce and bake in 400° oven for 20-25 minutes. Remove to heated platter and serve.

Suggested Wine: Letour de By—a red médoc.

Poached Halibut with Egg Sauce
Serves 4

  4 8 ounce halibut steaks
  1 cup whole milk
    Salt and freshly milled pepper to taste
  2 tablespoons butter
  2 tablespoons flour
  2 hard boiled eggs peeled and chopped finely

Place halibut steaks in a greased baking dish. Dust with salt and freshly milled pepper. Pour milk in and bake 18-20 minutes in 400 degree oven. Remove from oven and strain milk into bowl. Melt butter in 1-qt. saucepan and stir in flour. Cook until golden (roux), add milk and stir constantly until thick and smooth, adjust seasoning, then add chopped egg. Remove fish to serving platter and pour egg sauce over all. Dust with paprika and fresh parsley sprigs and serve.

Scallops and Mushrooms in Pastry

1 pound scallops
½ pound fresh mushrooms, sliced
½ cup Half and Half cream
⅓ cup dry white wine
¼ cup finely chopped parsley
1 teaspoon salt
½ teaspoon freshly ground pepper
½ pound frozen bread dough
Egg wash (1 egg yolk beaten with a little water)

Cut large scallops into quarters and smaller scallops into halves, then mix scallops and mushrooms together carefully. Combine the cream, wine, parsley and seasonings in a small mixing bowl. Roll out prepared dough on a heavily floured surface to about ⅜-inch thickness. Cut into eight 7-inch circles, then fit the circles into 4½-inch tart pans. Divide scallop mixture equally into the pastry-lined tart pans, then spoon the cream mixture over the scallop mixture. Gather the edge of the dough in each tart pan and pinch together over the scallop mixture, making a frill at the top and leaving a small hole in the center. Brush dough with Egg Wash. Bake in a preheated 400° oven for 25 minutes. Remove from tart pans to serve.

Suggested Wine: California Rhine Wine—cold and alive.

Crabmeat Sir Thomas

Serves 4

¾ pound butter
4 ounces ham—chopped finely
1 pound Alaskan King crabmeat, cut up coarsely
4 slices of white bread, crusts removed and made into bread crumbs
6 ounces good Swiss cheese, shredded

Melt butter in a heavy skillet and sauté ham until slightly crisp. Add crabmeat and warm through. Turn into a casserole large enough to hold. Combine bread crumbs and shredded cheese and top the ham and crabmeat. Place under broiler until cheese melts and the color is a rich golden brown. Serve piping hot.

Suggested Wine: Soave Bolla well chilled.

Lobster in Avocado Shells

Serves 4

2½ pounds shelled raw lobster
2 ripe avocados, pitted
2 limes
2 teaspoons dark brown sugar, packed firmly
8 ounces small, cooked, shelled and deveined shrimp
¾ cup red pimiento
1 clove garlic minced finely
1 ounce Parmesan cheese
3 ounces dry white wine
1 teaspoon dill
2 tablespoons butter
2 tablespoons clarified butter
Freshly ground pepper

Rinse lobster under cold water and dry thoroughly with a clean cloth. Finely dice pimiento. Mince the clove of garlic. Measure all liquid and dry ingredients and set aside. Remove pits from avocados by cutting through skin and flesh lengthwise. Scoop out pits at last possible moment. Squeeze limes and pour juice over avocados to prevent discoloration. Preheat broiler.

With a fork mash through the avocado flesh to the skin. Place avocado halves under the preheated broiler for about two minutes. Cut lobster into bite size pieces (remember lobster shrinks when cooked . . . so keep pieces a little large). Then pour clarified butter into a large frypan, over high heat, and add lobster meat. Season with pepper. Add no salt. Stir in brown sugar giving a sweet glaze. Remove avocado halves from under the broiler and set in a warm place. Stir tiny shrimp into frypan. Add pimiento and garlic. Pour wine into pan, shaking pan constantly. (There might be a moment of flame . . . let it, but be careful.) Add dill and stir in. Stir in 2 tablespoons butter and take pan off heat, allowing butter to melt into "sauce." Spoon this mixture into broiled avocado halves and sprinkle lightly with Parmesan cheese. Place under broiler, fairly close to heat source, for about 3 minutes, or until cheese is golden brown. Serve with lemon wedge.

Suggested Wine: Cafe de Bourg White

Jewish Sweet and Sour Fish

Serves 8

4½ pounds fresh trout, cleaned and filleted
  Pinch of salt
2 cups cider vinegar
½ cup water
½ cup light brown sugar
3 tablespoons butter
  Generous pinch of each: ground cinnamon and cloves
4 medium onions, peeled and sliced thinly
6 lemons, peeled and sliced thinly
1 cup seedless raisins
¼ cup sliced and blanched almonds
3 egg yolks

Salt the trout fillets slightly and keep refrigerated for 2 hours. Meanwhile, combine water, vinegar, brown sugar, raisins, butter and almonds with seasonings and boil until raisins are plump. Arrange the sliced onions on the bottom of a heavy Dutch oven. Cut the trout into 2-inch pieces—rinse under cold water to wash away excess salt. Place fish and lemon slices on top of onion base in pot. Pour in enough water to cover halfway up the fish fillets and simmer 15 minutes. Then add sweet/sour sauce and simmer an additional 30-45 minutes. Carefully lift out fish and turn heat to high and reduce sauce to half. Arrange fish on a deep warm platter. Strain the sauce. Beat egg yolks and stir into sauce gradually (do not boil—sauce will curdle!). Pick out as many raisins and almonds as possible from strainer with a fork—add to sweet/sour sauce and pour over fish. Let cool and serve with lemon wedges.

Stuffed Shrimp Josef
Serves 4

1 pound shrimp (under 15's) shell on
3 tablespoons butter
1 cup sweet onion, finely chopped
1 pound crab meat
⅓ cup Townhouse crackers, crushed finely
½ pint heavy cream
1 teaspoon sugar
Salt and freshly milled pepper to taste

Carefully split backs of shrimp, devein and rinse clean under cold water, drain well.

In a 1-quart saucepan, sauté onion in melted butter. Add crab meat and continue to sauté 2 minutes. Add heavy cream, sugar and cracker meal and stir to thicken about 10 minutes over lowest possible heat.

To stuff—spoon a generous amount of crab dressing into pocket created by splitting the back of the shrimp. Place in baking dish. Sprinkle with a little paprika and pour a little water into bottom of dish. Bake at 450° oven for about 10 minutes.

Suggested Wine: A Pinot Chardonay or champagne.

Barbecued Shrimp Oriental
Serves 4

1 pound fresh or frozen raw shrimp—shelled and deveined
⅓ cup peanut oil (salad oil will do)
¼ cup sherry wine
¼ cup soy sauce
2 cloves of fresh garlic, crushed
¼ teaspoon fresh ginger root, crushed and minced fine
¼ teaspoon paprika for color
Pinch cayenne pepper
Salt and freshly milled pepper to taste

Combine all liquid and dry ingredients to create barbecue sauce. Place cleaned raw shrimp into marinade and allow to stand 30-45 minutes, lightly tossing once in a while. Drain shrimp and thread on skewer. Place on broiler rack and cook 6 inches from heat source about 4-5 minutes. Baste often with soy-sherry marinade. To serve leave on skewer and place on lettuce-lined platter with lemon wedges.

Suggested Wine: A red jug wine.

Baked Fillet of Sole Tarragon

Serves 4

 8 very small (2 ounce) white fillets of sole
 1 cup bread crumbs
 4 tablespoons butter, melted
 3 shallots, peeled and minced or 3 green onions chopped and 1 clove minced garlic
   Salt and freshly milled pepper to taste
 ½ cup dry vermouth wine
 2 tablespoons tarragon
 1 tablespoon cold butter
   Juice of ½ lemon

Preheat oven to 425°.

Combine melted butter and bread crumbs until slightly moist. Bread sole with buttered crumbs and place in a shallow baking dish. Season with salt and fresh pepper. Sprinkle chopped shallots on and around fish. Pour enough vermouth into baking dish to half submerge fish (do not soak the bread crumbs atop the fish). Dust with tarragon and place in the hot oven. Bake for 30 minutes. Remove brown fish to platter. On a burner reduce juice to ½ volume—add lemon juice and cold butter. Serve with sauce on the side.

Suggested Wine: White Burgundy is luscious here.

Elegant Scalloped Oysters

Serves 6

1½ quarts of shelled oysters in their liquid
 2 cups crushed Townhouse crackers
 ¾ cup melted butter
 ¾ cup light cream
   Salt and freshly milled pepper to taste
   A dash (or 2) of Worcestershire sauce
 2 tablespoons dry sherry wine

Cover the bottom of a shallow baking dish or casserole with ½ of the crushed crackers. Combine oysters in their liquid, Worcestershire sauce, salt and pepper in a bowl and mix well. Pour over crackers in casserole. Sprinkle the remaining 1 cup of crushed crackers on top. Dribble melted butter over crackers and allow to absorb. Sprinkle with dry sherry wine and pour light cream over all. Wait 2 minutes, then bake at 350° for 25-30 minutes or until golden brown.

Suggested Wine: Wagner Serval Blanc.

Fish and Ham Rolls
Serves 4

    2 pounds fresh haddock fillets
      Salt and freshly milled pepper to taste
    1 teaspoon paprika
    3 tablespoons good grated cheese (Romano or
      Parmesan or a blend of both)
    2 teaspoons finely chopped fresh parsley
    1 teaspoon dry dill weed or 2 teaspoons finely
      chopped fresh dill
    4 thin slices of boiled ham
    1 tablespoon vegetable oil

Cut the fish into 4 equal pieces and sprinkle with the salt, pepper, paprika, grated cheese and herbs. Roll each piece of fish in a slice of ham, secure with a toothpick. Brush the rolls with the vegetable oil and broil for approximately 15 minutes, turning the rolls once halfway through the cooking time.

Remember, when you secure any roll with toothpicks, set the roll seam side down for the first part of the cooking to insure the meat will set in the shape of the roll.

To serve, remove the toothpicks and set the rolls on a warm platter, garnish with a sprig of fresh parsley or dill.

A nice variation is to prepare a white wine sauce and serve it on the side.

Suggested Wine: Any extra dry or Brut white wine—a Graves is beautiful!

Baked Scrod New Orleans
Serves 4

    2 pounds fresh Boston scrod
    2 tablespoons melted butter
      Salt and freshly milled pepper to taste
      Tomato sauce*
    8 lemon wedges

Place scrod into a shallow baking dish and brush with melted butter. Sprinkle with salt and fresh pepper. Pour creole sauce over fish and bake in a 400° oven for 20-25 minutes, or until fish flakes easily with fork. Remove to serving dish and garnish with lemon wedges and serve.

Suggested Wine: Soufard St. Emellion red.

Halibut with Herbs, Riviera
Serves 4

    4 8-ounce halibut steaks
    ¼ cup butter
      Sprigs of parsley
    3 shallots (green onions will do) finely chopped
    ¼ teaspoon dried thyme
    1 bay leaf
    ¼ teaspoon fennel seed
    1 carrot, grated
    1 lemon, thinly sliced
    8 (or more) Greek black olives, pitted and
      chopped
      Salt and freshly milled pepper to taste
    2 teaspoons lemon juice
    ½ cup dry sherry
    2 tablespoons fine dry bread crumbs
    1 tablespoon butter
    2 tablespoons finely chopped parsley

Dry the fish thoroughly with toweling and be sure it's completely thawed. Melt the butter in an ovenproof dish large enough to hold the fish steaks. Add fish, the parsley sprigs, shallots, thyme, bay leaf, fennel, carrot, lemon slices, and olives. Season the fish with the salt and pepper to your taste. Sprinkle the fish and herbs with the lemon juice and pour in the wine. Cover the dish with foil tightly and bake in a 400° oven for about 25 minutes to a half hour (or until fish is done). Remove from oven and turn to broil. Meantime, sprinkle the fish lavishly with the bread crumbs, dot with the butter, and broil until golden brown. Dust with the chopped parsley and serve hot.

Poached Fillet of Sole Victoria
Serves 4

    8 small fillets of sole
      Court bouillon*
    8 teaspoons minced lobster or shrimp meat
    4 teaspoons minced fresh mushrooms
      Sauce mornay*
      Grated Parmesan cheese

Fold the fillets of sole in half. Poach the folded side in enough court bouillon to just cover. Remove from poach and carefully place in an ovenproof dish. Garnish the top of each with 1 teaspoon of minced seafood meat and ½ teaspoon minced fresh mushrooms and bathe with a small amount of sauce mornay. Sprinkle with cheese and place under broiler until bubbly and browned slightly. Serve.

All'Antinore Herbed Shrimp in Beer

Serves 4

- 2 pounds peeled raw shrimp, deveined
- 1 cup beer
- 2 tablespoons lemon juice
- 3 cloves fresh garlic, peeled, crushed and minced
- 2 tablespoons fresh chives, chopped finely
- 2 tablespoons fresh parsley, chopped finely
- Salt and freshly milled pepper
- Shredded lettuce (iceberg)
- 2 green onions, finely minced for garnish

Marinate the shrimp in the beer, lemon juice, garlic, chives and parsley overnight. Next day . . . drain and reserve the marinade. Butterfly the shrimp by cutting down the back but not through, and open flat. Broil the shrimp until cooked and tender . . . maybe 5 minutes. Do not turn (less time for small shrimp, of course). In a fry pan, heat the marinade and reduce. Remove the shrimp to a heated platter on which you have made a foundation of shredded lettuce, spoon some of the sauce over and dust freely with chopped green onion. Use remainder of the sauce for dipping.

Suggested Wine: Cold Beer!!

Fillets de Soles Florentine

Serves 4

*Basic Mornay Sauce

Poach 4 sole fillets (until transparent color disappears) in equal parts white dry wine and water to which you add celery leaf, onion slices and a few peppercorns.

Cook 2 packages frozen or 1 pound fresh spinach and drain well. In a small skillet, melt 3 tablespoons butter and add a few slices of fresh garlic. When garlic begins to turn color, add spinach and sauté 2-5 minutes or until heated through.

Serve fillets on foundation of spinach and spoon Mornay Sauce over all.

Suggested Wine: Chablis.

Shrimp with Sesame Seeds and Spices

Serves 4

  3 tablespoons sesame seeds
  1 small clove of fresh garlic, peeled and sliced
  2 tablespoons oil
    A generous pinch of the following spices:
      cinnamon, ground cloves, chili powder
  ¾ cup chicken stock
    Salt and freshly milled pepper
  2 tablespoons lemon juice
  2 pounds cooked, shelled and deveined shrimp

Combine garlic slices, sesame seeds and oil in a heavy saucepan and sauté until sesame seeds are light brown. Remove from heat and stir in all the spices. Scrape into the container of an electric blender and add salt, pepper and chicken stock; blend to a sauce consistency. Return to the saucepan, add the lemon juice and heat over low heat, stirring in just one direction until thickened. Arrange the hot shrimp on a warm platter and spoon sauce over. Garnish with chopped green onions if desired and serve.

Suggested Wine: A California dry white wine complements this shrimp dish.

Shrimp à la Vienna

Serves 4

  2 pounds fresh shrimp, peeled and deveined
  2 shallots (or 1 medium onion), peeled and
    minced
  2 or 3 cloves fresh garlic, peeled, crushed and
    minced finely
  ¼ cup oil
  ¼ cup brandy
  ½ cup white wine
    A generous pinch of sugar
  1 teaspoon tomato pureé (optional)
    Salt and cayenne pepper to taste
  1 tablespoon butter
  1 tablespoon flour

Heat oil in a heavy fry pan and fry the onion and garlic; when soft, add the shrimp and stir fry for 2 minutes; add brandy and set aflame. After flame has burned itself out, add the wine, sugar, salt and cayenne pepper and simmer for 3 minutes. Blend soft butter with flour and tomato paste and add to the fry pan after removing shrimp. Stir briskly to thicken the sauce, replace shrimp in gravy and serve in a shallow bowl.

Suggested Wine: Brut Champagne.

Shrimp in Tarragon Wine Sauce

Serves 6

   2 green onions, finely chopped
   2 green peppers, finely chopped
   2 cloves garlic, crushed
   2 tablespoons butter
   2 pounds raw shrimp, shelled
   ½ teaspoon tarragon
   2 medium tomatoes, peeled and chopped
   ¼ teaspoon each salt and fresh milled pepper to
     taste
   2 tablespoons lemon juice
   ½ cup white wine
   ¼ cup white vermouth
   1 tablespoon cornstarch dissolved in
     2 tablespoons cold water
   2 tablespoons parsley, finely chopped

Cut shrimp through back leaving tail. Sauté green onions, green pepper and garlic in hot butter until soft. Add shrimp, increase heat to high, and cook 3 minutes. Add tarragon, tomatoes, salt and pepper, lemon juice, both wines and simmer for 5 minutes on lowered heat. Add cornstarch paste, simmer until thickened. Garnish with parsley and serve in a shallow bowl.

Suggested Wine: White Terlano of Italy.

Baked Flounder with Oyster Sauce

Serves 4

   4 fresh flounder fillets (6 ounces each)
   ¾ cup dry white wine
     Salt and freshly milled pepper to taste
   1 cup court-bouillon*
  30 oysters and their juices
   2 tablespoons flour
   2 tablespoons butter
     Juice of ½ fresh lemon

Marinate fish fillets in 8 tablespoons wine, dash of salt and fresh pepper for 30 minutes in a shallow baking dish. Bring the 1 cup of court-bouillon to a simmer and add the fish and gently poach for 10 minutes. Transfer the fish back to the shallow baking dish. Simmer the oysters in their own liquid for 5 minutes in a small saucepan. Make a roux with butter and flour—add oyster juice, ¾ cup of court-bouillon and the lemon juice and cook until smooth. Arrange the oysters on the fish—spoon sauce over and bake at 350° for 10-15 minutes.

Sautéed Shrimp with Chives and Gorgonzola Cheese
Serves 4

    2 pounds medium shrimp, peeled and deveined
    6 tablespoons butter
    ⅓ cup fresh parsley, minced
      Salt and freshly milled pepper to taste
      Generous pinch of paprika
    ⅓ cup dry sherry wine
  3-4 ounces Gorgonzola cheese (or bleu), crumbled
    ⅓ cup fresh chives, minced (¼ cup freeze dried
      chives)
    8 slices of toast, crust removed and halved
      (toasted points)

Heat butter in large heavy skillet and stir-fry
shrimp until they start to curl and turn
pinkish in color. Add parsley, season with salt
and fresh pepper, and dust with paprika.
Cook, stirring a couple minutes longer (do
not overcook shrimp—they'll be tough!).
Add sherry wine, chives and cheese—heat
through and toss gently to melt cheese.
Serve piping hot on toast.

Suggested Wine: Seyval Blanc—possessing
an aroma of fresh apples—crisp, fresh and
fruity.

Shrimp and Eggplant Sauté
Serves 4

    8 ounces of medium-size shrimp, cooked and
      shelled
    ½ cup sweet onion, peeled and chopped
    3 cloves of fresh garlic, peeled, crushed and
      minced
    ¼ cup butter
    1 firm eggplant (about 1 pound) peeled and
      soaked in salted water 20 minutes
    1 8-ounce can of whole tomatoes, drained and
      chopped
      Salt and freshly milled pepper to taste
      A good pinch of thyme
    ½ cup dry white wine (dry sherry is best, as far
      as I'm concerned)
    1 green pepper, seeded and chopped

Cut the shrimp in half lengthwise and set
aside. Melt the butter in a heavy skillet (be
sure it's large enough to hold the entire
entrée) and sauté the onion, garlic, and
green pepper until tender but not browned.

Shrimp and Eggplant (continued)

Cut the already peeled eggplant into bite-size pieces and add to the mixture already in the fry pan. Simmer for a minute then add the chopped tomatoes, salt and freshly milled pepper, season with a generous pinch of thyme and cook until the eggplant is tender (maybe 10 minutes). Stir in the cooked shrimp and stir fry until heated through, add the sherry or dry wine and simmer for 5 minutes longer.

Suggested Wine: Spain: a dry red Rioja

Scampi Con Prosciutto Maria Francesca
(Shrimp with Prosciutto Ham)
Serves 4

    16 medium shrimp, peeled and deveined (leave
       tail intact)
       Flour
    16 very thin slices prosciutto ham
     1 teaspoon dry leaf oregano
       Olive oil
     2 cloves of garlic, peeled, crushed and minced
    ¼ cup dry white wine
       Juice of ½ lemon
     2 tablespoons butter
       Chopped fresh parsley

Reconstitute dry oregano with 3 tablespoons olive oil and let stand. Wrap each shrimp in a slice of ham and set aside. Add some oil to a heavy skillet and barely warm minced garlic—add ham-wrapped shrimp and turn a few times to coat and flavor. Spoon oregano-oil mixture over shrimp and fry. Allow ham-wrapped shrimp to brown a little. Pour off oil and add wine to pan. Simmer 2 minutes to reduce and then add lemon juice and butter. Make a roux in a small saucepan of oil and flour (1 teaspoon each)—add to shrimp pan and stir in gently to thicken lemon butter sauce. Remove to a warm platter. Pour sauce over shrimp, dust generously with chopped fresh parsley and serve.

Suggested Wine: Pinot Blanc—you will note a faint hint of melon; what a complement to prosciutto and shrimp.

Baked Halibut Steaks Kalamata

Serves 4

 4 halibut steaks (6 ounces each)
   Salt and freshly milled pepper to taste
   Juice of 1 fresh lemon
 3 onions, peeled and sliced thin
½ cup water
 3 tomatoes, cut into eight wedges
¾ cup olive oil
 4 whole clove spikes
 1 cup raisins
 1 cup sherry wine
 8 lemon slices

Soak raisins in the sherry until plump. Steam onions in a deep heavy skillet in the ½ cup water. When the onions are tender, add tomatoes, olive oil, cloves and raisins with the wine and simmer over low heat for 15 minutes. Spoon some of the onion mixture into a shallow baking dish. Sprinkle the fish steaks with salt, fresh pepper and lemon juice and arrange side by side on the onion-tomato foundation. Spoon remainder of "sauce" evenly on top of each steak. Place 2 lemon slices on each steak and place in a 400° oven and bake open for 30 minutes. Remove carefully to a heated platter with the sauce and serve hot.

Suggested Wine: Liebfraumilch, maybe Blue Nun—a good middle of the road Rhein with some character.

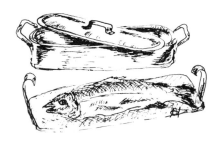

Meat

Beef

Veal

Pork

Poultry

Lamb

Variety Cuts

Meaty Gossip

Meat doesn't have to be graded by the U.S. Department of Agriculture in most states, that's the law! The grading by the USDA is voluntary and paid for by the meat industry (of course, in the long run—we pay). As a result—and you take note—only the top grades of meat at the market carry the blue-purple seal of the USDA. Beef is the most popular meat so we notice it more—but lamb, veal and pork can carry the stamp as well. Grades have been broadened lately, so that telling the difference between them (unless they're a grade apart) can be difficult.

Veal like lamb, is usually about three months old—but the younger the better. The best is "milk-fed" or never having been weaned or permitted to graze on grass. Of course there are two varieties of meat—the younger and whiter the more expensive and tender and desirable. The darker they become in color (to red), the older. Older lamb or veal can be made tender by marinating in lemon juice or milk. As either contains very little fat, it should always be cooked with some fat or liquid, and seldom broiled.

The chance of pork causing trichinosis today is "infinitesimal," according to the USDA. So the old cookbook methods suggesting overcooking or cremation can be re-evaluated. The trichina parasite is killed at 137° F (which is medium rare), but for best results at the table, you should go beyond this temperature and serve pork pinkish.

Pork like poultry has countless applications in the kitchen. Use both freely, creatively and carefully, for the least expensive culinary tour of the world imaginable.

Sliced Tenderloin Triestina

Serves 4

12 thin slices of tenderloin pounded thin
 2 tablespoons butter
¼ cup coarsely chopped onion
 1 cup sliced fresh mushrooms
½ cup artichoke hearts (quartered)
 1 cup cooked asparagus tips
¼-½ cup dry white wine
 2 more tablespoons butter
½ teaspoon sage
 1 cup brown sauce*
 2 teaspoons grated Romano cheese
    Salt and freshly milled pepper to taste

In a large heavy skillet sauté onions until lightly browned, add mushrooms and continue to sauté for 3-4 more minutes. Stir in asparagus tips gently. Add half of the wine and simmer 5 minutes over low heat.

Season tenderloin with salt and pepper. In a second fry pan melt remaining 2 tablespoons butter to which sage is added and place tenderloin slices and cook to preferred degree of doneness. Add rest of dry wine and simmer a moment longer.

Remove warm vegetable mixture to serving platter and top with sliced tenderloin and keep warm.

To the tenderloin pan, add brown sauce and heat through. Pour over tenderloin and dust with grated Romano cheese.

Suggested Wine: Valpolicella—an attractive Italian red from Verone.

Beef and Black Olive Casserole, Morocco
Serves 6

    1 pound beef, cut for stew
    4 tablespoons olive oil
    2 cloves of fresh garlic, crushed
    6 stalks of celery—string fiber removed and
      minced
    ½ teaspoon crushed red pepper
      Salt and freshly milled pepper to taste
      Water
  1¼ cups pitted "Greek" black olives
      Juice of 1 lemon

Heat oil in a heavy dutch oven (with cover) and sauté garlic and beef together until browned evenly on all sides. Reduce heat to low, add spices and celery, season with salt and fresh pepper (add water enough to moisten). Cover and simmer for 1 hour. Add olives, stir, and simmer 20 minutes more. Add lemon juice, adjust seasonings and cook 5 minutes to finish. Transfer to a deep dish and serve.

Suggested Wine: Dar Bel Amri made in the Atlantic Coast of Morocco—Full and quite robust.

Austrian Beef Casserole with Beer
Serves 6

    1 pound beef cut for stew
    2 tablespoons butter
    8 slices of bacon
    2 medium onions, peeled and sliced
    2 cups water
    2 cups beer
    3 tablespoons cider vinegar
    1 tablespoon brown sugar
      Salt and freshly milled pepper to taste
    2 whole clove spikes
    1 bay leaf

Melt 2 tablespoons butter in dutch oven (with cover) and sauté beef until brown on all sides—remove from pot. Line the pan with slices of bacon and place onion slices on top of bacon. Replace cubed beef on onions, add liquids, sugar and spices. Cover and bring to a good boil. Reduce heat to low and simmer for 2-2½ hours. Remove to appropriate deep dish and serve.

Suggested Wine: Barolo—a deep flavored dry red from Northern Italy.

Tenderloin Tips with Watercress Sauté

Serves 4-6

- 2 tablespoons cornstarch
  Enough peanut or vegetable oil to cook in
- 1 pound tenderloin tips or tender beef, cubed
- 2 egg whites
  Salt and freshly milled pepper to taste
- 2 teaspoons fresh ginger root, minced (same amount candied ginger)
- 3 cloves of fresh garlic, crushed and minced
- 2 small bunches of scallions, cleaned and chopped (greens too!)
- 1 cup fresh mushrooms, sliced
- 5 tablespoons sherry wine
- 1 tablespoon soy sauce—a teaspoon vinegar
- ½ teaspoon each—Cayenne and crushed red pepper
- ¼ —½-pound fresh watercress—coarsely chopped

Dissolve the cornstarch in cold water (enough to create a watery paste). Combine egg whites, salt and pepper, some oil and cornstarch paste in a bowl. Add tenderloin tips and mix thoroughly with your hands.

In a second small bowl, combine sherry wine, ginger, soy sauce and vinegar, more fresh pepper. While you're at it, make a paste of cayenne and crushed pepper mixed in a few drops of oil in small bowl No. 3.

Put enough oil in a heavy skillet or wok to provide ¼-inch cooking depth and over high heat, stir-fry the cubed beef for about 20-30 seconds or until all red color is gone from surface of meat. Add garlic and scallions and fry for another minute—add the sherry-soy mixture and stir 2 or 3 times (use wooden spoon). By now the beef should be barely browned outside and medium rare inside. Add pepper mixture and continue to stir for 15 seconds, then add mushrooms and watercress. Remove (after a stir around to heat mushrooms and wilt watercress) with a slotted spoon to a hot platter.

Suggested Wine: A dry red wine from Spain's Rioja region—excellent red table wine.

Tenderloin of Beef Krejcik (Polish)

Serves 8

    3 pounds beef tenderloin
      Salt and freshly milled pepper to taste
    2 tablespoons Dijon mustard
    ¼ pound butter
    1 pound pork roast, coarsely ground
    6 fresh mushrooms, coarsely chopped
    1 small onion, peeled and minced
    1 medium (¾ to 1 pound) head savoy cabbage
    1 tablespoon fresh parsley, chopped
    1 egg
6-8 slices of bacon

Rub the tenderloin with salt, pepper and mustard and refrigerate for 2 hours. Peel 8 outside leaves from savoy cabbage and save—core and shred the rest. Brown the tenderloin in ½ the butter and let cool a little. Meanwhile, sauté ground pork, onion, mushrooms, shredded cabbage and chopped parsley—let cool. Combine the ground pork-vegetable mixture with egg—season to taste. Lay out reserved cabbage leaves (overlapping) on a flat surface. Place browned tenderloin on leaves. Spread ground pork-vegetable mixture over the meat and wrap in cabbage leaves. Place "roll" seam side down in an ovenproof dish. Cover with bacon slices and dribble any butter left in fry pan over and bake in a 400° oven for 20-30 minutes. Allow to rest 10 minutes. Remove to a warm platter and serve—carving at the table.

Suggested Wine: Red Graves—a serious wine of Bordeaux, but very complementary to this Polish entrée.

Norwegian Seaman's Stew

Serves 4

- 8 thin slices of beef round
- 3 tablespoons butter
- 2 medium onions, peeled and sliced ½-inch thick
- 8 potatoes, peeled and sliced ½-inch thick
  Salt and freshly milled pepper to taste
- 2 cups of ale or beer

Melt the butter in a dutch oven and brown each steak on both sides—removing each as it is done and keep warm. Sauté onions in the same butter until soft and transparent. Season onions with salt and fresh pepper. Layer meat, onions and raw potatoes alternately in the Dutch oven (season each layer with salt and fresh pepper). Add the ale and simmer for about an hour or until the potatoes are done (pass a skewer through the layers and touch bottom of pot to test for doneness).

Suggested Beverage: Beer or cold ale.

Steak Diane All'Antinore

Serves 4

- 4 thin slices of beef for steak
- 4 tablespoons butter
  Salt and freshly ground pepper to taste
- 1 medium onion, peeled and chopped
- 2 gloves of garlic, peeled, crushed, and minced finely
- 1½ teaspoons sharp French mustard
- 1 teaspoons Worcestershire sauce
- 3 tablespoons brandy
- 3 tablespoons each white wine and heavy cream

Beat the steaks gently to flatten and sauté in a heavy skillet using melted butter. (Cook to your liking but stop short of complete, as you are to place the steaks over heat again!) Season with salt and freshly ground pepper and remove and keep warm. In the same fry pan, sauté the onion and garlic until tender, add mustard and mix well . . . then add Worcestershire sauce and stir. Replace the steaks and flame the brandy over steak. When flames subside, add the white wine and cream and heat almost to boiling point . . . serve hot.

Suggested Wine: 1966 Pomerol—a firm Bordeaux, rich and fruity.

Beef with Red Wine and Olive Sauce

RED WINE AND OLIVE SAUCE
 Combine in the blender and blend until smooth:
  ½ cup green olives, pitted and coarsely chopped
  ½ cup fresh orange juice
  8 anchovy filets, coarsely chopped
  ½ cup pimientos, coarsely chopped
  2 cloves garlic, peeled and cut in pieces
  2 shallots (or small onions), coarsely chopped
  1 cup tomato juice
  1 cup dry red wine

BEEF
  4 tablespoons olive oil
  2 pounds of lean shoulder of beef (or 1½ pounds of hip beef) cut in 1-inch pieces
    Salt and freshly milled pepper to taste
  ½ teaspoon oregano
    Chopped parsley

This entreé may be made on top of the stove or in the oven. Preheat oven to 375° if you prefer this method of cooking.

Select a large, heavy, heatproof casserole; heat the olive oil until it begins to sizzle. Put the beef in hot oil and sauté all sides until lightly brown. Cover the beef with the wine-olive sauce. Mix in salt, pepper, and oregano.

Cover and put in oven (375°) for 2 to 2½ hours, or over low simmering heat on top of the stove for the same period of time. When the meat is tender, skim off the fat from the top of the sauce. One advantage of making this sometime in advance is that the fat rises to the top and is more easily removed when cold. Serve it generously sprinkled with chopped parsley.

Suggested Wine: St. Julien—the epitome of a well balanced red wine.

Porterhouse Steak à la Cacciatora
Serves 2

  1 tablespoon olive oil
  1 large porterhouse steak about 1½ inches
    thick
    Salt and freshly milled pepper
  4 tablespoons sherry wine or Marsala wine
  ½ cup dry red wine
  2 cloves of garlic, peeled and crushed
  ½ teaspoon fennel seeds
  1 tablespoon tomato paste mixed in 3
    tablespoons water

Heat the oil in a heavy skillet and fry the steak on both sides to just under your preference and add salt and fresh pepper. Remove from pan and keep warm. Add the sherry to the pan juices and cook slowly, scraping the pan for the bits of food on the bottom, until the wine has almost evaporated. Add garlic, fennel, tomato paste and red wine and cook two minutes longer, mixing with the pan gravies. Pour over the steak when ready to serve.

Suggested Wine: A cool Beaujolais Villages.

Belgian Stew with Pears
Serves 6

  12 small pears, halved and cored
    Pinch of tarragon
  2 pounds of beef for stew
  2 tablespoons oil
  6 cups beef stock*
    Salt and freshly milled pepper
  4 medium potatoes, peeled and cut up

In a heavy saucepan, stew the pear halves with the pinch of tarragon for about ¼ hour over very low heat. Meanwhile, in a second dutch oven, sauté the beef stew in oil until brown on all sides—season with salt and freshly milled pepper. Add stock and simmer meat for 1½ hours or until tender. Add potatoes 20 minutes before beef is done. Drain the pears. Place beef stew on a heated platter. Garnish with pears and serve.

Suggested Wine: Rosé D'Anjou—nice!

Stuffed Beef Rolls in Brandied Cream Sauce

Serves 4

- 1 pound of fresh mushrooms, wiped clean and sliced
- 8 tablespoons butter
  Pinch of thyme
- 6 ounces chicken livers
- 6 bay leaves
  Salt and freshly milled pepper to taste
- ½ cup of brandy
- 2 hard boiled eggs
- 12 thin slices of beef round for braciola
- 12 slices of bacon
  Flour
  Enough beef stock* to half cover the rolls of beef
- ¼ cup heavy cream at room temperature

Melt 3 tablespoons butter in a heavy skillet. Sauté the chicken livers with 1 bay leaf—season with salt and fresh pepper to taste and add the brandy. Cook until the brandy has almost evaporated and the livers are tender. Transfer livers to a chopping bowl and sauté mushrooms until very tender in 2 tablespoons butter. Add to livers, along with the hard boiled egg and chop together to almost a paté. Carefully flatten the beef slices with the heel of your hand or the side of a cleaver. Place a slice of raw bacon on each and a dollop of the liver paté in the middle. Roll the beef up, tucking in the edges. Attach two rolls together with a bay leaf sandwiched between with a toothpick. Melt the remaining butter in the large skillet and sauté beef rolls carefully—browning on all sides. Sprinkle with flour and turn over to coat with butter. Add remaining ¼ cup brandy and reduce to half. Add enough beef stock to half cover the rolls. Cover the pan and simmer for an hour. Remove the tender rolls carefully to a heated platter and remove toothpicks and discard bay leafs. Add the cream, raise the heat and reduce to a slightly thickened sauce. Adjust seasonings and pour sauce over beef rolls, reserving some for the table.

Suggested Wine: Cote de Beaune Villages—a lovely Burgundy, delicate & fruity—well flavored red.

Sliced Tenderloin Beef with Summer Savory (France)

Serves 6

2 pounds beef tenderloin, sliced thinly
2 tablespoons butter
½ pound fresh mushrooms, wiped off and sliced
3 small onions, peeled and sliced thinly
1 clove fresh garlic, peeled and sliced thinly
1 tablespoon paprika
½ cup red wine
½ cup beef broth*
½ teaspoon summer savory
Salt and freshly milled pepper to taste
1 tablespoon chopped fresh parsley (garnish)

Melt butter in a heavy skillet until very hot (don't burn) and sauté meat slices, onion and garlic until lightly browned. Remove meat only. Add savory, wine, paprika, broth and season with salt and fresh pepper and reduce the sauce to ½ its original volume. Add sliced mushrooms and heat through. Place meat on warm platter—pour all of sauce over and garnish with freshly chopped parsley. Serve.

Suggested Wine: Morey-St. Denis "Burgundian nobility!" Wonderful dry red wine.

Ćevapćići (Yugoslavian Beef Fingers)

6-8 servings

2 pounds lean ground beef
3 eggs, beaten
Salt and freshly milled pepper
3 tablespoons fresh green pepper, seeds removed and minced very finely
1 medium onion, peeled and minced finely

Combine ground beef with eggs, salt and fresh pepper and mix well. Shape into thumb-sized "fingers." Skewer and charcoal grill until done (10-15 minutes over low coals), turning frequently to brown on all sides. (Bake during winter or bad weather in 425° oven turning often.)

Mix raw pepper and onion together. Serve Ćevapćići piping hot with raw vegetable in a separate side dish.

Suggested Wine: Ćvićek—the traditional light red wine of Slovania.

Tyrolean Alps Beef Stew
Serves 6

    2 cups brown sauce*
    3 tablespoons butter
    2 cups fresh sliced mushrooms
    2 medium onions, peeled and chopped
    1 clove fresh garlic, peeled and minced
    2 pounds beef tenderloin cut for stew
    ¼ cup dry sherry wine
      A couple dashes Worcestershire sauce
      A dash of bitters (optional)
      Salt and freshly milled pepper
      Steamed white rice

Heat the butter in a large heavy skillet and sauté the onion and garlic until soft, push aside and add the meat. Fry until browned on all sides, add the mushrooms and continue to cook. After meat is browned, add the brown sauce, dry sherry, Worcestershire sauce, bitters and season to taste. Heat for 5 to 10 minutes and serve over the fluffy white rice.

Suggested Wine: A California Cabernet Sauvignon.

Austrian Style Goulash
Serves 6

    6 tablespoons oil or butter
    6 medium onions, peeled and sliced
    3 pounds beef cubed for stew (chuck, shoulder
      or tenderloin tips)
    2 teaspoons paprika
    1 tablespoons vinegar
      Caraway seeds and leaf marjoram to taste
    1 cup beef stock
    1 tablespoon flour blended into 1 tablespoon
      soft butter

Fry onions until soft and transparent, add the beef cubes and brown. When brown on all sides, add paprika, vinegar, caraway and marjoram and a dash of salt and freshly milled pepper; mix well and continue to sauté a minute longer. Add the beef stock and simmer until beef is tender (2 to 3 hours); when done, add the flour-butter paste (roux) and blend well to create a thick gravy and boil a few minutes before serving. This is best if cooled and stored overnight and reheated slowly and served the next day!

Suggested Wine: A red wine from the Alsace region—or a Beaujolais.

Turkish Beef Casserole with Olives and Walnuts

6 servings

       6 ripe tomatoes
1½ pounds rump steak
       2 cloves garlic
       2 tablespoons olive oil
          Salt and freshly milled black pepper
       6 ounces ripe stoned olives
½ cup red wine
       1 cup broken walnuts

Plunge the tomatoes into boiling water for a few seconds and slip off the skins. Cut the beef into (1-inch) cubes. Crush the garlic and rub into beef cubes with salt and pepper to taste (use your hands to combine ingredients).

Heat oil and gently cook the tomatoes for 5-6 minutes, crushing them with a fork into a purée. Add meat, olives, wine and walnuts. Cook over a medium heat for 20 minutes, stirring occasionally.

Suggested Wine: Pino Noir or young Beaujolais (slightly chilled).

Meat Loaf à la Diavalo

Serves 6

1½ pounds lean ground beef
    1 cup bread crumbs
    4 tablespoons prepared mustard
    2 tablespoons horseradish
    1 small onion, chopped finely
    1 or 2 cloves fresh garlic, crushed and minced
    2 teaspoons Worcestershire sauce
½ cup bottled chili sauce
       A dash of cayenne pepper...more if you like it
       Salt and fresh pepper to taste
    1 egg, beaten
¼ cup dry red wine

Combine all ingredients in a large enough bowl to allow room for kneading. Knead the ground beef mixture for 3-5 minutes, turning the mixture over several times. Shape the blended meat into a French bread loaf shape and bake in an open pan for 40 minutes at 400°. Baste a few times during baking to get a nice crisp-browned crust. Cool for 10 minutes before serving for easier and cleaning slicing.

Suggested Beverage: Beer or ale.

Steak Au Poivre All'Antinore

Serves 4

- 4 sirloin steaks, 8 oz. each
- 6 tablespoons clarified butter
- 2 teaspoons rosemary leaves
- 2 teaspoons sage leaves
  Rock salt (kosher salt)
- 3 ounces cognac
- 6 ounces heavy cream—room temperature
- 5 tablespoons veal stock (light beef stock will substitute)*
- 2 teaspoons Dijon mustard
- 2 teaspoons sour mustard
  Coarsely ground black pepper to taste

Beat steaks to flatten a little, season with salt and press roughly crushed pepper into each side of all steaks.

Heat butter in a large fry pan and when hot add rosemary and sage. Remove herbs after ½ minute, otherwise they will burn. Place steaks in the dry pan and brown quickly on each side. Pour heated cognac over steaks and light with a long stick match. (It will flare briefly, then burn blue; be careful!)

Remove steaks from the pan, and keep warm on a serving platter. Into the cooking pan add veal stock and when warm, stir in heavy cream to deglaze. Stir mustards into sauce with black pepper to taste. Bring to a boil, pour over steaks and serve.

Make sour mustard by adding 1 teaspoon vinegar to 2 teaspoons prepared mustard.

Suggested Wine: A big Burgundy!

German Pork and Beef Casserole with Cabbage

Serves 4

  1 small head of white cabbage
  1 tablespoon oil
  2 medium onions, peeled and chopped
  ½ pound lean pork, cut for stew
  1 pound lean ground beef
  1 teaspoon caraway seeds
    Salt and freshly milled pepper to taste
  ½ cup dry white wine
  1 teaspoon oil
6-8 thick slices bacon

Remove tough outside leaves from cabbage and core. Place the whole head into a large pot ½ filled with boiling water. Simmer 10 minutes. Remove and drain well. Carefully remove 10-12 leaves and set aside. Chop the remaining cabbage.

In a heavy skillet, heat the 1 tablespoon of oil and fry the onion, pork stew and ground beef until lightly browned. Pour off excess fat. Add the chopped cabbage, caraway and season (salt and fresh pepper). Pour the wine over, cover and simmer for 10-15 minutes, stirring often.

Lightly grease an ovenproof dish with the teaspoon of oil and line the dish with half the cabbage leaves. Spoon the sautéed mixture into casserole and cover with the remaining 6 leaves (tuck down the sides for a neat appearance). Arrange the bacon on top and place in a 400° oven. Bake (open) for 30 minutes and serve in the casserole piping hot.

Suggested Wine: Schillerwein— a light red from near Württemberg, Germany.

Bavarian Supper Casserole in a Skillet

Serves 4

    4 6-ounce cube steaks
    1 tablespoon oil
    1 medium onion, peeled and chopped
 *2 cups brown sauce
    ½ cup sliced fresh mushrooms
    2 tablespoons brown sugar
    2 tablespoons vinegar (cider)
    1 teaspoon caraway seeds
    3 cups shredded cabbage
    2 potatoes, peeled and cubed

In a large heavy skillet brown the cube steaks in the hot oil. Add onion and cook until almost tender. Meanwhile, combine the brown sauce, caraway seeds, brown sugar, and vinegar in a bowl. To the onion and steaks, add the sliced mushrooms and stir for a moment, then add the sauce mixture; cover and simmer for 15 minutes. Skim off any fat.

Cook the shredded cabbage and diced potatoes in a separate saucepan in a little salted water until tender. Drain and remove vegetables to a warm serving platter as a foundation. Place steaks atop the cabbage and potatoes and spoon the rich sauce over all. Reserve some sauce for the table and serve on the side.

Suggested Wine: Yugoslavian Cabernet Savignon.

Czechoslovakian Braised Tenderloin with Vegetables & Sour Cream

Serves 4

    4 thin slices of tenderloin
    ¼ pound bacon
      Salt and freshly milled pepper to taste
    2 tablespoons flour
    1 medium onion, chopped
    1 small carrot, peeled and "coin" cut
    1 small parsnip, peeled and Julienne cut
    ½ small celery root, peeled and chopped
    2 cloves of fresh garlic, crushed and minced
      Generous pinch of allspice
    ½ bay leaf (if old—use whole leaf)
    1 tablespoon vinegar
    1 cup sour cream
    1 tablespoon flour
    ½ cup white wine

Flatten tenderloin slice with heel of hand, season with salt and pepper and dredge in flour.

Sauté ½ of bacon in a heavy skillet over high heat—add tenderloin and fry quickly on both sides. Remove and set aside. Add remaining bacon and vegetables. Sauté until lightly browned. To the vegetable mixture, add the bay leaf, allspice, vinegar, and meat. Simmer for 5 to 8 minutes. Remove everything from pan with slotted spoon. Mix the last tablespoon flour with the sour cream and blend into the pan juices thoroughly. Strain and return to the pan—add vegetable/meat mixture and wine and simmer for 2 minutes.

Suggested Wine: Bulgarian Donau Perle— pale and a trifle sweet

Greek Beef Stew with Eggplant

Serves 6

    3 pounds of beef, cut for stew
    2 medium eggplants, peeled and cut into round slices (soak eggplant in salted water for 20 minutes)
    3 medium onions, peeled and coarsely chopped
    2 cloves of fresh garlic, peeled and sliced thinly
    ½ pound butter
    5 firm ripe tomatoes, cut into eighths
      Salt and freshly milled pepper to taste
      Water as needed

Greek Beef Stew (continued)

In a heavy Dutch oven with cover, melt half the butter and fry the beef stew until evenly browned. Season with salt and fresh pepper. Add onions and garlic and sauté until onions are soft and transparent. Add tomato wedges and simmer until puréed. Pour 1 cup of water into the pot and continue simmering after a stir to mix all ingredients. Remove eggplant from water—pat dry and sauté in a heavy skillet using the remaining butter. Place cooked eggplant on top of meat, season again lightly, cover and simmer over low heat 20 minutes longer (most of the liquid will be absorbed). Remove to appropriate dish and serve.

Suggested Wine: Aloxe-Corton—a good dry red table wine.

Armenian Beef with Quince and Dill
Serves 6

    1 pound beef, cut for stew
    2 tablespoons bacon fat or 6 slices of bacon,
        cut up
        Water
    1 pound quinces, peeled, cored and sliced (held
        in lemon and water) (tart apples will sub)
    1 medium fresh onion, peeled and sliced thinly
        Olive oil or butter
        Salt and freshly milled pepper
    1 tablespoon (or less to your taste) dill weed

Sauté the bacon in a heavy Dutch oven (with cover) until fat runs. Add stew beef and brown lightly on all sides. Add only enough water to cover the meat, cover and simmer over low heat for an hour. Drain the quince (or tart apple) and add to meat. Sauté the onion in olive oil or butter in a small fry pan—add to stew meat and quinces. Season with salt and fresh pepper to taste. Recover and simmer until meat is very tender. Spoon into a deep serving dish—dust with dill weed and serve.

Suggested Beverage: Beer.

Tournedos of Beef Tenderloin ala Zia Maria Guiseppa

Serves 4

- ¼ pound butter
- 8 3-ounce filets mignon (center cut tenderloin steaks)
- 1 clove fresh garlic, crushed and minced
- ¼ cup canned roasted peppers with their oil, chopped
- 2 cups sliced fresh mushrooms
- ½ cup dry white wine
- ½ cup beef stock*
- 1 tablespoons butter and 1 tablespoon flour for roux
- 2 ounces brandy
  Salt and freshly milled pepper to taste
  Chopped fresh parsley

Melt most of the butter in a heavy skillet and sauté meat to rare—remove and keep warm (it'll keep cooking while warm). Add remaining butter and sauté garlic and roasted peppers with their oil, add mushrooms and stir-fry about 2 minutes. Add wine, beef stock and roux, stirring until sauce thickens (it won't be a very thick sauce) and simmer for 10 minutes. Replace meat and simmer until warm through. Season, add brandy and remove to a warm platter. Pour sauce over meat. Dust with parsley and serve.

Suggested Wine: A good Pommard ('64).

Weiner Schnitzel

Serves 2

- 2 ½-inch thick veal cutlets
  Salt and freshly milled pepper
- 1 egg
- ¼ cup fine bread crumbs
  Oil to cook in
  Juice of 1 lemon and 4 thin lemon slices
  Parsley bouquets for garnish

Pound the veal cutlets, season with salt and fresh pepper. Beat the egg until frothy and dip the veal into the egg first, then into the fine bread crumbs. Heat the oil in a heavy skillet (be sure to have only enough to cover the bottom of the pan). Sauté the veal over low heat for about 10 to 15 minutes a side . . . it must be served crisp! Dribble a little lemon juice over just before serving and garnish with fresh parsley bouquets and lemon slices.

Suggested Wine: A good Rhine wine—chilled and spicy.

Beef Tournedos Orientale
Serves 4

- 8 3-ounce beef tenderloin or ribeye steaks (marinade: place steaks in a bowl and sprinkle with salt, freshly milled pepper, soy sauce and a little pinch of ground ginger for 15 min.)
- 4 tablespoons whole butter
- 1 cup sliced mushrooms
- 1 clove garlic, crushed and minced
- ½ cup water chestnuts, sliced
- ½ cup bamboo shoots
- 1 small pkg. frozen pea pods, (thawed, not cooked)
- 3 ounces bean sprouts—smallest can on market shelf
- 8 seasoned slices of bread (croutons toasted in butter)

In a wok or heavy skillet sauté garlic and marinated steak in butter to desired doneness. Remove and keep warm. In the same pan add mushrooms, water chestnuts, pea pods, bamboo shoots and bean sprouts. Stir-fry vegetable mixture for 2 minutes.

Place each steak on a toast crouton and spoon vegetables on top.

Veal Cutlets with Sour Cherry Sauce All'Antinore
Serves 4

- 4 lean veal cutlets, about 6 ounces each
- 2 tablespoons butter
  Salt and freshly milled pepper to taste
- ¼ cup red wine
- 2 tablespoons evaporated milk
- ½ pound canned sour cherries, drained well
  Parsley bouquets for garnish

Dry the cutlets. Heat butter in a heavy skillet and sauté the veal to evenly brown on both sides (3 minutes per side). Season with salt and fresh pepper on both sides, remove from pan and keep warm. Blend wine and evaporated milk in the fry pan and simmer for 3 minutes—scrape the bits to deglaze. Add the cherries and heat through. Return the cutlets to pan and reheat (do not boil!). Arrange cutlets on warm serving platter and pour cherry sauce on. Garnish with parsley bouquets and serve.

Suggested Wine: France's most famous Rosé, Tavel—a little strong and dry, leaning toward orange color.

Veal Stew with Ham and Mushrooms

Serves 6

1¼ pounds boneless veal (cut from the leg)
  3 teaspoons heavy cream—room temperature
  2 lemons
  6 slices smoked ham, thinly sliced
    Veal or beef stock* to moisten
  6 asparagus spears
    Zest of half a lemon
    Worcestershire sauce
  8 ounces fresh mushrooms
  3 tablespoons white wine
  2 tablespoons flour
  2 tablespoons onions, diced
  3 tablespoons butter
  6 ounces grated cheese
    Sliced lemon
    Salt and freshly milled pepper

Cut the veal into small cubes and cook covered for 45 minutes in the stock with the diced onions and a little salt. Make a roux with the butter and flour, blend in the veal stock and boil to a very thick sauce. Blend in the cream and stir in the juice of 1 lemon, salt, pepper, the lemon zest and a little Worcestershire sauce. Cook the mushrooms under cover in a little lemon juice with a pinch of salt, add to the sauce together with its cooking liquid, add the cooked veal, then cook for 5 minutes, stirring constantly. To serve in individual portions, cover the bottom of 6 small fireproof dishes with a slice of ham. Place equal amounts of stew on top and decorate with small pieces of asparagus. Sprinkle liberally with grated cheese and brown well in a hot oven or under a salamander. Serve in the dish garnished with a slice of lemon.

Suggested Wine: Verdicchio dei Castelli de Jesi—A wine of ancient Etruscan origin—fresh and pale white with a distinct character.

Veal Sauté alla Matta

Serves 4

- 8 veal escallopes, cut very thin (2 ounces each)
- 1 small eggplant, peeled, diced and soaked in salted water 20 minutes
- 3 tablespoons olive oil
- 2 cloves fresh garlic, peeled and sliced thin
- ¼ pound of bacon, cut small
  A pinch of oregano
  Salt and freshly milled pepper to taste
- 3 ounces of grated Romano or Parmesan cheese (a blend of both is good)
  Flour
- 6 tablespoons butter
- 4 tablespoons Marsala wine
  Parsley bouquets for garnish

Pound the escallopes of veal as thin as possible without mashing. Dain the eggplant and rinse clean of salt, pat dry. Heat the olive oil in a heavy skillet and add the garlic slices and sauté until very fragrant, lightly brown and sweet . . . discard. Fry the cut up bacon in the garlic oil until crisp, remove to paper toweling to drain. Add the eggplant and quickly brown in the same pan, seasoning with salt, fresh pepper and a pinch of oregano. Mix the eggplant and bacon together in a bowl. Pour off oil and add butter. Sauté the veal until nicely brown on both sides after you have dredged it through flour lightly. Add the wine and move pan back and forth until sauce thickens. Replace the bacon-eggplant mixture and heat through; adjust seasonings. Simmer 2 minutes then remove the meat and vegetables to a warm platter. Garnish with fresh parsley bouquets and a generous dusting of grated cheese.

Suggested Wine: Chianti Classics di Italia

Danish Meat Patties

Makes 8-10 Patties

- ½ pound pork and ½ pound veal ground fine (or ½ pound lean ground beef)
- 1 medium onion, coarsely chopped
  Salt and freshly milled pepper to taste
- 3 tablespoons flour
- 4 tablespoons butter
- 3 tablespoons vegetable oil
- 1½ cups club soda (or sparkling mineral water)
- 1 egg, well beaten

Danish Meat Patties (continued)

In a large mixing bowl, beat the flour into the ground meat with a wooden spoon (or hands); add coarsely chopped onion and blend into mixture. Gradually add club soda a few tablespoons at a time until the meat takes on a "fluffy" texture. Thoroughly beat the egg with salt and pepper and add to meat mixture. Cover the bowl with foil or plastic film wrap and let rest refrigerated for 1 hour. (This will firm up the meat and make it easier to handle.) Shape the ground meat mixture into finger shapes and set aside. Melt the butter with the oil over high heat, in a heavy skillet. When melted and foamy, lower the heat to medium and fry the "fingers" (4 or 5 at a time, don't crowd) for about 6-8 minutes, turning often to insure browning on all sides. When cooked, remove to a warm platter, continue until all patties are done.

Suggested Wine: A good California Varietal Zinfandel.

Escallops of Veal Curry

Serves 6

    3 tablespoons butter
   12 slices of lean veal
    2 onions, sliced thinly
    1 clove garlic, chopped finely
      Mix together a generous pinch of: cumin, dry
      mustard, cayenne pepper, turmeric, coriander,
      ground ginger, salt and freshly milled pepper
      in small bowl. (These five spices comprise the
      curry.)
   ½ cup water
      Juice of ½ lemon
    4 tablespoons flour

Dredge veal escallopes through flour to lightly coat. Melt butter in a heavy skillet—place veal escallops, garlic and onion around and sauté until veal loses its pinkish color and onions are soft. Sprinkle the curry over veal-onion mixture, coating veal with the spices and simmer 2-3 minutes longer. Add water and shake pan gently back and forth to create a curry sauce. Add lemon juice and shake pan a few more times to blend—serve with hot boiled rice.

Suggested Wine: An excellent Fino sherry.

Veal Rolls à la Lyonnaises

Serves 6

    6 thin slices of veal
    4 ounces bacon
    ½ cup chopped parsley
    1 clove garlic
      Salt and freshly milled pepper
      Pinch each of four spices (crushed pepper,
      cloves, ginger, and nutmeg)
    6 tablespoons butter
    1 sliced carrot
    1 sliced onion
 1¼ cup dry white wine
 1¼ cup hot strained stock
    1 sprig thyme
    2 bay leaves
    1 teaspoon cornstarch
    1 tablespoon cold water

Trim the edges of sliced veal to make them neat and even. Mince the veal trimmings with bacon, parsley, and garlic. Season to taste with salt and pepper, sprinkle in four-spice mixture and blend well. Put a tablespoon of this stuffing on each slice of veal, roll up and secure with fine kitchen string.

Melt half the butter in a saucepan, put in carrot and onion. Add veal rolls and cook. When the paupiettes (rolls) start to stick, pour the wine over them. Allow the sauce to come to a boil once, add stock, thyme and bay leaves. Check seasoning, add more salt and pepper, if necessary. Cover and simmer gently for 30 minutes. Remove strings. Keep paupiettes hot. Rub the sauce through a sieve or pass through a blender. Heat remaining butter in a saucepan, add 2 tablespoons of the sieved sauce. Dilute cornstarch with cold water and stir into the pan. As soon as the mixture begins to thicken, add the rest of the sauce. Bring to boil and put in veal rolls. Finish off in the oven preheated to 475° for 10-15 minutes. Remove to warm platter and serve.

Suggested Wine: Rosé d'anjou

Veal Piccata with Parsley

Serves 4

    8 veal scallops, cut thin
      Salt and fresh black pepper
      Flour
    6 tablespoons butter
      Juice of ½ lemon and 1 wedge
1½ tablespoons fresh parsley, finely chopped

Place the veal scallops between sheets of waxed paper and pound as flat as possible with the side of a cleaver, or meat mallet. Sprinkle each side of veal with a pinch of salt and pepper and dredge through flour (light coat only). Melt 4 tablespoons butter in a large, heavy skillet and brown the veal a few slices at a time, over fairly high heat. Arrange the browned veal slices overlapping slightly on a preheated serving platter and keep warm. Break up remaining 2 tablespoons butter into the skillet with juices of veal and cook over brisk heat until "sauce" has turned golden brown; add lemon juice, reduce heat and stir for a few minutes to thicken naturally. Spoon the sauce over the veal slices and dust lavishly with chopped parsley. Serve immediately with lemon wedge squeezed over all.

Suggested Wine: Castelli Romani, a "tart" red table wine from Italy.

Escallops of Veal with Artichokes Marie Louise

Serves 4

    8 escallops of fresh white veal
    4 teaspoons butter
      Flour
½ teaspoon marjoram
    8 cooked artichoke hearts (canned)
½ cup dry white wine
    2 or 3 shallots or onions, chopped finely
      Salt and freshly milled pepper to taste
    6 anchovy fillets, chopped finely (optional but good!)
      Juice of ½ lemon
¼ cup each of pitted Greek olives and green olives, chopped
    1 tablespoon Parmesan cheese

Escallops of Veal (continued)

Dredge veal through flour. Melt butter in a large heavy skillet and sauté floured veal for 3-4 minutes or until browned on both sides. Add salt and pepper, marjoram, artichoke hearts, shallots, anchovy fillets, chopped olives, wine and cheese. Gently stir until the veal is coated well and lower heat to simmer . . . cook for a few minutes until sauce thickens. Serve on a foundation of wide noodles and add a few strips of pimiento for color.

Suggested Wine: Margaux 1966. Expensive, but worth it!

Veal Transylvania All'Antinore
Serves 6

- 2 pounds of veal, cut for stew
- 2 tablespoons flour
- 3 tablespoons butter
- 3 tablespoons oil
- 2 large onions, peeled and chopped
- 3 potatoes, peeled and thinly sliced
- 2 green peppers, seeded and sliced
- 2 small zucchini squash, sliced
- 3 tablespoons chopped fresh parsley
- ½ pound fresh mushrooms, sliced
- ¼ pound fresh green beans, ends snipped and cut in half
  Salt and freshly milled pepper to taste
- 4 firm, ripe tomatoes, sliced
- ½ pint sour cream

Dredge cubed veal in flour and sauté in oil and butter in a heavy casserole until lightly browned. Add onions and fry with veal until soft and browning. Remove from heat. Add potato and zucchini slices, pepper slices, parsley, salt, fresh pepper and green beans—toss to mix. Place sliced tomatoes on top—cover and bake in 350° oven for 1 hour. Remove from oven and uncover. Stir in sour cream and raw mushrooms and serve in casserole.

Suggested Wine: Baco Noir—an Eastern states red wine—best if older—deep and full bodied.

Sliced Veal Sauté with Ham
Serves 4

       5 tablespoons butter
       2 cloves of fresh garlic, crushed and minced
    ½ cup cooked ham, diced
       1 cup fresh mushrooms, quartered
          A bit of celery leaf
       8 2-ounce each slices of veal round . . . be sure
          the slices are thin
          Flour
          Salt and freshly milled pepper to taste
    ½ cup dry white wine
    ¼ cup Sauce Demi-Glace*
    12 stuffed Spanish olives
       4 hard boiled eggs, quartered

Melt the butter in a heavy skillet and add
garlic and diced ham. Sauté the two for 3
minutes, then add the celery leaf and
mushrooms. Continue to fry for 2 minutes
and push aside in the skillet, making room
for the veal. Dredge the veal in the flour to
lightly coat, place slices into the fry pan and
sauté until all pink color is gone. Sprinkle
with salt and pepper to taste. Add all the
wine to pan and deglaze by shaking the pan
back and forth over heat. Now add the Sauce
Demi-Glace, the olives and the quartered
eggs. Do not stir to mix; instead gently shake
the pan back and forth until everything has
blended and thickened.

Suggested Wine: Valpolecello.

Dana Ve Potlacan (Turkish)
(Veal and Eggplant)
Serves 4

       2 3-ounce slices of veal per person
       1 large eggplant, sliced and quartered (1-inch
          thick), soak in salted water 20 minutes
       4 medium firm tomatoes, cored and sliced
    4-6 cloves garlic, crushed and minced
       3 medium onions, sliced
    ½ cup beef or veal stock
          Salt and freshly milled pepper to taste
       1 bay leaf
          Cooking oil
          (optional: 1 yellow or zucchini squash sliced
          and quartered and ¼ cup freshly chopped
          parsley)

Heat cooking oil, enough to nicely cover bottom of heavy skillet and sauté veal slices. Remove from pan and keep warm. Add more oil (¼ cup) and fry eggplant for 5-7 minutes. Add minced garlic, onion, tomato (squash and parsley) and season to taste. Turn down heat and simmer vegetables until tender. Drain off ½ of pan liquids, add veal stock and simmer 5 minutes. Replace veal slices and continue to simmer 2 minutes. Serve like a stew dusted with fresh parsley.

Suggested Wine: Dry red.

Escallops of Fresh Veal with Mushrooms and Egg
Serves 4

    8 2-ounce veal escallops cut Italian style
      Flour
      Salt and freshly milled pepper
      Butter
    1 pound fresh mushrooms, wiped clean and
      sliced
    2 green onions, chopped finely (including green
      portion)
    1 clove garlic, peeled and halved
    3 eggs
    1 tablespoon chopped fresh parsley
    4 thin slices of fresh tomato
      Grated cheddar cheese to garnish

Pound veal thin and dredge lightly through flour. In a heavy skillet melt enough butter to sauté veal. When lightly browned, reduce heat and continue to sauté with garlic halves for 2-3 minutes. Remove garlic and veal— discard garlic. Keep veal warm. Add mushrooms and chopped green onions to pan and sauté until mushrooms begin to get tender (2 minutes).

In a bowl beat eggs, season with salt and fresh pepper—mix in parsley. Scramble with mushrooms and onions until just set. Spoon the egg mixture evenly over the 8 pieces of veal. Cover each crowned veal escallop with a half slice of tomato and sprinkle with cheddar cheese. Place in a 400° oven for 3-5 minutes or until cheese melts. Serve!

Suggested Wine: Lambrusco Salamino de Santa Croce. A pleasant red wine with a fruity bouquet but acidic wine.

Veal Stew Sauté Champignon

Serves 6

2½ pounds veal, cut for stew
  4 tablespoons butter
  4 tablespoons flour
  1 pound fresh mushrooms, sliced
  ¾ cup Marsala wine
  1 clove fresh garlic, crushed and minced
     Fresh parsley, snipped for garnish

In a large bowl sprinkle flour over veal stew meat and toss to coat evenly.

Over medium high setting melt the butter in a heavy sauté pan or skillet. Carefully place floured veal stew pieces into hot butter (it will splatter some) and sauté 5-7 minutes, stirring occasionally. Add sliced fresh mushrooms and continue to sauté for 3 minutes.

Sprinkle this mixture with minced garlic and stir once.

Pour the Marsala wine into the sauté pan all at once. Be careful as it might flame! Slide the pan back and forth over burner to mix well and thicken sauce. Turn the heat down to low setting and simmer 5 minutes.

Remove to a warm serving platter and dust with snipped parsley.

Suggested Wine: Sparkling Burgundy—New York State

Calf's Liver Kashmir

Serves 4

  3 tablespoons butter
  4 4-ounce thin slices of fresh calf's liver
     Flour—seasoned with salt and freshly milled pepper
  3 cups thinly sliced fresh onions
  8 ounce container plain yogurt
  3 teaspoons ground ginger
     Thinly sliced orange for garnish

Heat the butter in a heavy skillet and sauté onions until soft and transparent. Lightly dredge liver slices through seasoned flour. Place liver in fry pan with onions and continue to fry until liver begins to brown (turn once). Combine yogurt and ginger and mix well—add to pan. Cover and simmer 15 minutes on lowest possible heat. Stir from time to time to keep from sticking.

Remove to a warm platter and garnish with orange slices. Serve.

Veal Scallopini with Onions

Serves 4

- 12 2-ounce veal cutlets, Italian style
- 2 tablespoons olive oil
- Salt and freshly milled pepper
- 1 teaspoon minced fresh thyme (or ¼ teaspoon dry leaf thyme)
- 2 cloves garlic, peeled and minced finely
- 2 large onions, peeled and sliced
- ⅓ cup dry sherry wine
- 1½ cups chicken stock*
- 2 tablespoons butter

Pound the veal very thin with meat mallet. Place olive oil in a heavy skillet over high heat. Sprinkle cutlets with salt and fresh pepper and sauté until lightly browned. As cutlets shrink during cooking, push aside and add more to pan. Remove meat from pan when browned and keep warm. Brown juices in pan until water evaporates (2 minutes). Add thyme, onions and garlic and sauté until onions become soft but not brown. Add sherry and chicken broth—deglaze pan by scraping bottom with wooden spoon. Reduce heat and simmer to reduce stock (10 minutes). Add butter to onion sauce, adjust seasoning and spoon over veal on platter. Serve.

Suggested Wine: Est! Est! Est!

Veal Cutlet All'Antinore

Serves 2

- 4 veal cutlets, about 2 ounces each, pound thick
- 1½ teaspoon paprika (1 teaspoon for dusting, and ½ for sauce)
- Salt and freshly milled pepper to taste
- Flour
- 2-3 tablespoons butter
- 2-3 shallots (or onion) chopped finely
- ¼ cup dry white wine
- ½ cup beef stock*
- Grated rind of ½ lemon
- ¼ cup heavy cream
- 1 teaspoon dill weed and 4 bouquets of fresh parsley

Veal Cutlet All'Antinore (continued)
Sprinkle both sides of veal with salt, pepper and 1 teaspoon paprika and dredge through the flour. Shake off excess. Melt butter in a heavy skillet and sauté veal over medium heat until browned on both sides. Remove from heat. To the pan juices add shallots, beef stock, wine, lemon rind, and ½ teaspoon paprika. Turn the heat to simmer and stir for about 5 minutes or until sauce thickens. Remove from heat and add heavy cream slowly, stirring all the time. Return to heat and carefully heat through. Pour sauce over veal which was removed and keep warm. Sprinkle with the dill weed and garnish with bouquets of parsley.

Suggested Wine: Big Bordeaux Red

Veal Chops Sautéed with Bacon and White Wine

Serves 6

1 cup sliced bacon cut up into ½ inch pieces
2 tablespoons butter
6 thin shoulder veal chops
  Salt and freshly milled black pepper to taste
1 medium onion, chopped finely
2 cloves of garlic, crushed and minced
1 medium carrot, peeled and sliced very thinly
2 tablespoons chopped fresh parsley
2 tablespoons flour
1 beef bouillon cube dissolved in ¾ cup hot water (your own beef stock best)
¾ cup dry white wine
  Juice of half a lemon

Melt butter in a large heavy skillet and sauté bacon until it curls but does not brown. Add veal chops, season with salt and fresh pepper and continue to fry until both sides of veal and bacon are nicely browned. Remove chops and bacon from pan and keep warm. Pour off half the fat then add the finely chopped onions and garlic, sliced carrots and sauté until carrots are crisp-tender. Add parsley and stir. Continue to stir, add the flour and mix thoroughly (roux) . . . keep stirring. Add the beef broth and white wine to the pan and in a short time the sauce will thicken. Return the meat to the simmering pan, pour the lemon juice over all, stir once again . . . be sure it's all hot, remove to a platter and serve.

Suggested Wine: A Gewürztraminer—cool and spicy German white.

Veal Stew with Red Wine

Serves 6 to 8

    3 pounds veal, cut for stew
    ¼ pound butter
    2 onions, peeled and quartered
    4 tablespoons all purpose flour
    2 cups of red burgundy wine
    1 clove of garlic, minced finely
    1 bay leaf
    ⅛ teaspoon thyme leaf
    3 sprigs parsley
      Salt and freshly milled pepper
   12 small boiling onions
18-20 small mushroom caps
      A chunk of butter
    1 teaspoon sugar
    2 tablespoons Madeira

In a heavy dutch oven, sauté the veal in butter with the quartered onions until onions begin to brown. Stir in the flour and continue to cook a few minutes longer. Add all the burgundy wine, garlic, bay leaf, thyme and parsley. Set lid ajar and turn down heat to simmer for about 1 hour. Remove and discard bay leaf and parsley sprigs, adding salt and freshly milled pepper to taste.

Peel the small onions and place in pan of water—bring to a boil, drain and rinse. Brown these onions and the small mushroom caps in a fry pan with the chunk of butter. Add to the stew and continue cooking until veal is extra tender. When done, add sugar and Madeira, stir, taste, adjust seasonings and serve.

Suggested Wine: California Riesling.

Roast Veal with Green Peas à la Portugal

Serves 6

    3 pound boneless leg of veal (tied)
    3 tablespoons olive oil
      Generous pinch of thyme
    1 bay leaf
    4 cloves of fresh garlic, peeled, crushed and
      minced finely
      Pinch of ground cinnamon
      Pinch of saffron (optional)
    2 large tomatoes, peeled and chopped
      Salt and freshly milled pepper to taste
    3 tablespoons brandy
    ¾ cup dry white wine
    1 cup beef broth*
    2 tablespoons butter
    2 tablespoons flour
    2 tablespoons fresh parsley, chopped
    2 10-ounce packages frozen peas or 1 pound
      shucked fresh peas

Brown the veal in a heavy skillet in the olive oil. Then add the garlic, tomatoes, salt and fresh pepper, saffron, thyme, bay leaf and cinnamon and fry for 3-5 minutes more. Transfer to a casserole and add the brandy, wine and beef broth. Cover and bake in a preheated 400° oven for 1 hour or until veal is tender. Remove the veal to a warm platter. Make a roux with the butter and flour (use the empty skillet)—add to the casserole stock and stir to thicken. Add the parsley and peas and simmer for 5 minutes. Slice the veal on the serving platter and pour sauce over just before serving.

Suggested Wine: Bairrada—good sparkling wine or an exceptional red carafe wine.

Börek

Serves 8-12

    1 package filo pastry (frozen)
    1 whole egg beaten
      Salt and freshly milled pepper
      Granulated garlic—optional
    ½ pound feta cheese
    1 small bunch parsley (Italian style best)
      Melted butter
    1 egg yolk well beaten with water

Börek (continued)

Thaw filo dough and peel several leaves to stack. Crumble feta cheese and fold into whole egg. Chop parsley and blend into egg and cheese mixture. Salt and pepper to taste. Brush every 2 filo leaves with melted butter and stack (about 8-12 leaves high). Cut across rectangle (short side) to make 3″ wide strips. Spoon about a teaspoon of cheese mixture onto bottom left corner and fold triangular shape twice to seal in filling. Cut off. Repeat across strip until all strips are used. Brush triangles with butter and beaten egg yolk. Bake at 350° until lightly browned.

Roast Fresh Ham Kentucky Mint Julip

Serves 6-8

Pre-heat oven to 400°F.

    A 5-6 pound fresh ham
  2 cups dark brown sugar
  1 teaspoon dry mustard
  1 teaspoon prepared mustard
  4 tablespoons Bourbon whiskey
    Several whole clove spikes
  ½ cup white creme de menthe
    Juice of one fresh lemon
    Salt and freshly milled pepper
  1 large can of pears, drained

Place ham on rack in an open roaster and score ¼-inch deep with a sharp knife in a lattice design. Insert a clove spike at each intersection in the lattice. Place the ham into the hot oven and bake for 2 hours. Meanwhile, mix the sugar, mustards, and bourbon together, making a paste. After the first hour of baking, remove the ham from the oven and spread the bourbon-mustard paste evenly over the surface; return to the oven. After 30 minutes, remove again and pour the creme de menthe over all and add the pear halves and complete the remaining half hour of baking. Remove from oven and let sit and "rest" for at least 20 minutes. Set on a warm platter and present at the table for carving and serving. A garnish of pear halves, either minted in green creme de menthe or left as is, and fresh mint leaves can be added for color.

Baked Pork Chop with Fig and Apple Glaze

Serves 4

    4 10-ounce center cut pork chops
    1 can figs in heavy syrup
    2 fresh apples, peeled and sliced
    ¼ cup honey
      Juice of ½ fresh lemon
    ½ teaspoon dry mustard
    1 cinnamon stick
    ½ cup dry white wine
    1 small bunch green onion, chopped finely with
      green included

Preheat oven to 350°.

Dot each pork chop with ½ tablespoon butter and place butter side down in shallow baking dish. Add chopped green onion and bake pork chops 20 minutes. Meanwhile, combine wine, honey, cinnamon, mustard and lemon juice in a saucepan and heat to almost boiling. Add apple slices and fig juice. Simmer until bubbly and thick (apples will become tender). Remove from heat. Chop figs coarsely and add to sauce. Remove pork chops from oven—pour ½ fig-apple glaze over and return for 10 minutes more, or until chops are elegantly brown and sticky. Place on a warm platter and serve with reserved sauce to pass.

Suggested Wine: New York State Pink Catawba, chilled.

Orange Glazed Pork

Serves 4-6

    1 3-pound smoked, boneless, pork shoulder
      butt
    2 cans (6 ounces each) frozen concentrated
      orange juice, reconstituted
    ½ cup frozen concentrated orange juice, thawed
    2 tablespoons Dijon mustard
    ⅓ cup packed brown sugar
    ½ teaspoon ground cloves

Place pork in large kettle. Add reconstituted orange juice; cover and simmer for 1 hour. Remove pork from liquid and place in shallow baking pan. Combine undiluted orange concentrate with remaining ingredients; brush over pork. Bake in 400° oven for 45 minutes, basting with orange sauce every 15 minutes. Serve.

Brussels Sprouts with Sausagemeat Balls

Serves 4

1½ pounds frozen Brussels sprouts, thawed
4 slices of bacon cut into ½-inch pieces
   A pinch of salt and a dash of nutmeg
2 cups of fresh mushrooms
1 cup pork sausage meat
¼ cup dry white wine

Place the cut-up bacon into a heavy Dutch oven type pot and fry until the fat begins to run. Add the thawed brussels sprouts and sauté for 2-3 minutes or until they begin to brown. Add a pinch of salt and the nutmeg. Pour in the wine and simmer for 15 minutes. Meanwhile, form the sausagemeat into little meatballs and add to the simmering pot and cook for 5 minutes. Add the raw sliced mushrooms and stir into the stew.

Remove to an appropriate serving vessel. Serve in the European style soup bowls with plenty of French bread or crisp breadsticks.

Suggested Beverage: Dark beer or robust ale

Karelian Meat Stew

Serves 6-8

1 pound beef for stew
1 pound pork for stew
1 pound veal for stew
   Salt and freshly milled pepper
   Butter
2 bay leaves
2 large onions, peeled and chopped
   Hot water as needed
¼ cup red wine

Preheat oven to 400°.

Season the meat with fresh pepper and salt and knead in onions with a crushing action. Place meat in a butter greased casserole, add bay leaves and dot the top with butter. Pour wine in and add enough water to barely cover the meat. Cover and bake 1½ hours—remove the cover for the last half hour. Liquid should be reduced to a light gravy (if not, let cook longer) and the top of meat should be slightly browned.

Suggested Wine: Sylvaner—although a white wine, it complements here beautifully.

Pork with Ginger and Radishes

Serves 4

2½ pounds lean pork
 ¾ cup sliced radishes
 2 teaspoons finely minced garlic
 1 tablespoon soy sauce
 1 tablespoon brandy
 1 cup water
 1 tablespoon lemon juice
 1 large onion
   Vegetable oil
 2 teaspoons finely minced ginger root or
   1 teaspoon dry ground ginger
 1 tablespoon dark brown sugar
1½ tablespoons cornstarch
 1 cup beef stock*
   Salt and freshly milled pepper to taste

Remove all fat from pork and cut into julienne strips—¼ inch thick, and about 1-2 inches long. Slice onion. Be sure radishes are cut into thin slices (approximately ¾ cup in volume). Heat 2-3 tablespoons of oil in heavy skillet and sauté pork julienne strips until all pink color is gone—add onion, garlic and fresh ginger. Stirring constantly, continue to sauté for about 3 minutes more.

In a bowl, combine soy sauce, brown sugar, brandy, cornstarch and beef stock.

Boil water in a saucepan and pour over soy mixture. Stir and blend until smooth. Pour over meat in skillet and bring to a boil—turn down heat and simmer a few minutes. Stir in lemon juice, add salt and freshly milled pepper to taste and serve in a shallow dish piping hot!

Suggested beverage: Cold beer.

Hungarian Paprikash with Pork
Serves 6

1½ pounds pork, cut for stew (most of fat removed)
2 tablespoons lard or oil
2 large onions, peeled and chopped
2 cloves fresh garlic, peeled and crushed
1 tablespoon red paprika (Hungarian)
1 green pepper, seeds removed and sliced
2 medium tomatoes, cut into eighths
Salt and freshly milled pepper to taste
Water
½ cup sour cream
Stewed prunes with lemon wedges

Fry the onion and garlic in lard until soft in a heavy dutch oven (with cover). Add meat and brown evenly on all sides. Add paprika, sliced pepper, wedges of tomato, some salt and a little water (maybe 3 tablespoons). Cover—lower heat to lowest possible setting and simmer until tender . . . adding water a little at a time as needed. As soon as pork is tender, add the sour cream and bring to a boil. Transfer to a deep dish. Garnish with pitted stewed prunes and lemon wedges and serve.

Suggested Wine: Vilány—a Burgundy styled red made from pinot noir and very good.

Smoked Ham in Brandy Cream Sauce
Serves 4

1 pound smoked ham, sliced ⅛″ thick and cut into small cubes
3 tablespoons butter
2 cups half and half cream
2 tablespoons cornstarch
¼ cup milk
A good jigger Madeira Wine
2 ounces brandy

In a heavy saucepan, place ham and enough water to cover and bring to a boil. As soon as water boils, drain water off. Add butter to pan and melt over low heat. Add cream and very slowly bring to almost boiling (don't scorch!). Dissolve cornstarch into milk and add slowly to simmering cream, stirring constantly until sauce thickens (5 minutes). Add Madeira wine and brandy, salt and milled pepper to taste.

Serve over sliced hard cooked eggs placed on toast crouton for a first course—an elegant brunch entreé.

Orange Glazed Spareribs
Serves 4-6

4 to 5 pounds spareribs, cut in serving pieces
1 can (6 ounces) frozen concentrated orange
   juice
¾ cup ketchup
2 tablespoons molasses
1 teaspoon Worcestershire sauce
½ teaspoon tabasco pepper sauce
2 teaspoons salt
4 teaspoons grated onion

Place spareribs in large kettle; cover with water and bring to a boil. Reduce heat and simmer, covered for 30 minutes. Drain and refrigerate until ready to grill. Mix undiluted orange concentrate and remaining ingredients. Place spareribs on grill, set 6 to 8 inches from heat. Cook 15 minutes; turn and brush with orange sauce. If desired, garnish with halved orange slices.

Oven roast in open roasting pan at 400° procedure same as above.

Apples, Sausages and Sauerkraut All'Antinore
Serves 6

1 medium onion, peeled and sliced thin
2 tablespoons butter
½ pound each Polish-style sausage, knockwurst
   and bratwurst, sliced
1 large firm apple
4 tablespoons seedless raisins
3 tablespoons honey
   Paprika, salt and freshly milled pepper
1 1-pound can sauerkraut, drained and rinsed
¼ cup dry white wine

Melt the butter in a heavy skillet and sauté sliced onion until soft, push aside—add sliced sausages and brown on all sides with the onion.

While sausage mixture is cooking, peel and core the apple; cut into thick slices (top to bottom).

Remove sausage from frying pan and keep warm. Add the apple slices and raisins to pan and cook until apple is tender. Add honey, paprika, salt and fresh pepper. Stir, and add sauerkraut. Simmer for 3 minutes. Pour in wine, add cooked sausages and onion mixture, toss lightly and remove to warm serving platter.

Suggested Wine: A good fresh Riesling.

Ham Veronique

    4 slices of smoked ham
      Few slices of root vegetables for flavoring
      (onion, carrot, parsnip)
    2 bay leaves
    6 peppercorns
    1 cup dry white wine
    1 medium onion, finely chopped
 ½ cup soft butter
    6 tablespoons flour
1½ cups chicken stock
      Salt and freshly milled pepper to taste
    2 egg yolks
 ¾ cup heavy cream
 ½ pound white seedless grapes
      Chopped fresh parsley

Poach the ham steaks in water (just deep enough to cover) with the root vegetables, bay leaves and peppercorns for about 10 minutes over low heat. Boil the onion in the wine until reduced by about half. Melt the butter and add the flour to create a roux and cook for a few minutes. Add the chicken stock and bring to a boil. Meanwhile strain the wine and add to the stock. Season to taste. Pour a little of the sauce over the egg yolks and cream (which you have mixed together). Whisk back into the saucepan and reheat without boiling. Add the grapes, drain the ham and arrange on a platter with some of the sauce. Sprinkle with the parsley and serve with remaining sauce on the side.

Suggested Wine: A New York State dry white wine overchilled (cold).

New Jersey Pork Chops and Cranberry
Serves 4

    4 thick pork chops, lean
      Flour to dredge through
    2 tablespoons butter
    1 cup whole cranberry sauce (canned)
1½ tablespoons grated orange rind
 ½ cup crushed fresh pineapple (optional)
 ⅓ cup water if needed

Flour chops and fry in a heavy skillet until brown on both sides. Combine the remaining ingredients and pour over the chops; cover, reduce heat to low and simmer for an hour or until chops are very tender. Remove to a warm platter and serve.

Suggested Wine: Meursault a Côte De Beaune, a rich, smooth and mellow white.

Porco Assado Al'Asturiana

(Asturian Stuffed Pork Roast)
Serves 6

2 pound boneless pork loin
  Salt and freshly milled pepper
2 tablespoons olive oil
1 medium onion, peeled and chopped
2 cloves fresh garlic, peeled and crushed
3 tomatoes, peeled and chopped
1 teaspoon chili powder
8 black olives (Greek style), pitted and chopped
⅓ cup raisins
2 cups cooked rice
½ cup dry white wine
2 pounds potatoes, peeled
1 pound small boiling onions, peeled

Cut a "pocket" into the pork loin lengthwise and season with salt and fresh pepper. Heat the oil in a skillet and sauté onion and garlic until soft. Add tomatoes and chili powder and simmer for 5 minutes. Add the olives and raisins. Combine half the vegetable mixture with the cooked rice and fill the pocket ⅔ full. Press the pocket "closed" and tie to hold together (every 2-2½ inches). Roast the pork for 1 hour in a preheated 350° oven. Pour off excess fat. Add the remaining vegetable mixture—the potatoes and small onions and wine and cook 50 minutes to an hour longer or until pork and potatoes are tender. Baste often with the sauce during last half hour. Remove to appropriate serving platter. Spoon sauce over, slice and serve.

Suggested Wine: A dry sherry wine, chilled.

Bavarian Stuffed Pork Escallops

Serves 4

4 thick pork escallops
  Salt and freshly milled pepper
2 tablespoons rosemary
1½ teaspoons dry basil (1, if fresh)
4 ounces diced ham
1 medium onion, chopped
½ pound fresh mushrooms, chopped
1 tablespoon chopped parsley
2 teaspoons freeze-dried chives (or fresh)
4 tablespoons flour
2 eggs, beaten
3 tablespoons bread crumbs
  Vegetable oil

Bavarian Stuffed Pork Escallops
(continued)

Cut a pocket in each escallop of pork. Combine salt, pepper, rosemary and basil and dust the escallop inside and out.

Combine diced ham, chives, onion, parsley, mushrooms. Mix well and stuff the pork with the mixture. Secure open end with toothpicks (remove before serving, however). Dredge each stuffed escallop lightly in flour, then dip in egg and bread crumbs (pat lightly to insure even breading).

Heat vegetable oil (enough to cover bottom of heavy skillet). Fry escallops for about 8-10 minutes, on each side or until well done.

Place pork on a serving platter. Cut each escallop in half to show filling and serve.

Suggested Wine: Rosé wine of South America—a rosé is light yet strong enough for this entrée

Flemish Meatballs in Beer
Serves 4

> 2 slices of white bread, crusts removed
> 4 tablespoons milk
> 1 pound ground beef
> ½ pound lean ground pork
> 1 egg
>   Salt and freshly milled pepper to taste
>   Generous dash of nutmeg
> 6 tablespoons butter
> 2½ cups of beer
> 6 tablespoons flour

Soak the bread with milk and knead into the two ground meats—adding the egg, nutmeg and season to taste (salt and fresh pepper). Mix well and form into 8 meatballs. Sauté in 3 tablespoons butter until golden brown. Add the beer and simmer 20-30 minutes. Remove to a heated platter carefully. Add flour to remaining butter and cream. Add the flour mixture slowly to beer-batter and stir with a wire whisk until sauce thickens. Pour over meatballs and serve.

Suggested Beverage: Cold ale or beer.

Lomo De Cerdo Alentejo (Portugal)

(Loin chops of pork in wine sauce)
Serves 4

    8 tablespoons olive oil
    8 thin loin chops of pork (4 ounces each)
    2 cloves of garlic, peeled and crushed
5-8 peppercorns, crushed
    Flour seasoned with salt and freshly milled
    pepper
    1 onion, peeled and chopped finely
    ¼ cup dry white wine
    ¼ cup beef broth*
    1 tablespoon red wine vinegar

Marinate the pork chops in a marinade of 6 tablespoons olive oil, garlic, and crushed peppercorns in a shallow dish for 2 hours. Turn often to keep moist. Heat remaining oil in a heavy skillet. Sauté chops until brown on both sides. Remove to a warm platter. Add onions to oil and fry until soft. Add broth, wine and vinegar—scrape bits off bottom of pan to deglaze. Replace the chops in the liquid and simmer slowly, uncovered, for ½ hour—turning pork once after 15 minutes. When sauce is reduced, remove meat to platter, pour sauce over and serve.

Suggested Wine: A good dry white port (from Portugal, of course).

German Sausage Casserole

Serves 6

    Some vegetable oil
    1 pound sauerkraut lightly rinsed
    2 medium onions sliced
    1 tablespoon caraway seed
    ½ pound sausage (your choice, not Italian
    sausage) cooked
    Mashed potato—enough to cover

Sauté the sauerkraut, onion and caraway seed in the oil, using a heavy skillet. When onions are tender, alternate slices of cooked sausage in layers with sauerkraut mixture in a casserole. Top with mashed potatoes (frosting fashion) and bake for 15-20 minutes at 400° to heat through and brown potatoes. Serve in casserole.

Savory Braised Pork Chops with Chocolate Sauce

Serves 4

- ¾ cup of almonds, toasted and crushed
- 1 small clove of fresh garlic, crushed and minced
- 1 tablespoon olive oil
  A pinch of ground cinnamon
- 8 lean pork chops (4 ounces each)
  Flour
- 6 tablespoons butter
  Salt and freshly milled pepper to taste
- ½ cup dry sherry
- 1 medium onion, chopped
- ½ pound of mushrooms, wiped clean and sliced
  Beef stock to cover*
- 2 tablespoons grated milk chocolate

Further crush the toasted almonds with the minced garlic (make a paste-like mixture). Blend in the oil and season with the pinch of cinnamon. Dredge the pork chops in flour to lightly coat. Heat the butter in a large heavy skillet and sauté the pork chops (without crowding) until browned on both sides. Season with salt and fresh pepper. Add the wine—increase heat to high and reduce wine to almost nothing. Remove the chops and keep warm. Add a little more butter if needed and add onions and mushrooms. Cook for 2 minutes, then add the almond-garlic paste and stir-fry for 5 minutes. Add the cooked chops to pan and pour in enough beef stock to barely cover chops. Sprinkle with the chocolate—cover and simmer 10 minutes. Remove chops to a warm platter (keep warm) and continue cooking, stirring until sauce thickens. Pour chocolate-almond sauce over chops and serve. "You'll love it!" No wine with chocolate!

Roast Loin of Pork Nona Antinore

Serves 4

- ¼ pound butter
- 2 pounds of boneless pork loin, rolled and tied
  Salt and freshly milled pepper to taste
- 1 teaspoon dry leaf sage
- 2 pounds of fresh turnips, peeled and cut into small pieces
- 1 heaping teaspoon sugar
- 3 tablespoons red wine vinegar

Melt the butter in a large heavy skillet. Place the pork roast into a shallow roasting pan and pour 2 tablespoons of melted butter over. Season with salt and fresh pepper and sprinkle sage over. Place in a 350° oven uncovered. Add the small pieces of turnip to the remaining butter and sauté over high heat. As the turnips become tender, reduce heat and simmer until cooked through (they should be a nice golden brown color). Lightly season with salt and pour in vinegar. Increase heat and evaporate vinegar. After the roast has been in the oven for an hour, add the turnips and gently lift the roast and mix the turnips with the pan juices. Cook 20-30 minutes more or until the pork is beautifully browned and tender. Remove to a warm platter and let "rest" for 10 minutes. Slice and serve (you may want a sauce demi-glace* on the side to moisten meat).

Suggested Wine: Vino di Orvieto, Bianco Secco—full bodied and semi-dry (sweet) gorgeous with any roast pork entrée.

Ground Beef Sausage Egyptianne

Serves 4

- 1 pound ground beef
- 2 cloves fresh garlic, peeled, crushed and minced
  Salt and freshly milled pepper to taste
- 2 hard boiled eggs, shells removed and quartered
  Flour
- 2 eggs, beaten
  Bread crumbs
- 2 tomatoes, peeled and chopped
  Olive oil
- 3-4 fresh basil or mint leaves (½ teaspoon dry of either—NOT BOTH)

Ground Beef Sausage
Egyptianne (continued)

Tear a 12-inch-long piece of wax paper to work on. Spread ground beef into a 1-inch-thick, 10x3" loaf on lightly floured wax paper. Sprinkle with minced garlic and season with salt and fresh pepper to taste. Press the egg quarters (side by side) lightly into the meat and lift the wax paper to roll up to resemble thick sausage shape. Cut in half. Carefully roll sausage in flour and dip in egg and bread crumbs.

In a heavy skillet: Sauté chopped tomato in olive oil, add salt and fresh pepper and basil. When tomatoes have melted (become a pureé), add the sausage roll. Cover, reduce heat and cook 30 minutes turning only twice, very carefully. Remove to warm platter and serve.

Roasted Fresh Ham Ala Finland
Serves 4

    3 pounds lean fresh ham (boneless)
      Salt and freshly milled pepper to taste
    1 large tart apple, halved, cored and sliced
    1 medium onion, peeled and chopped
   10 cooked prunes, pitted
    1 tablespoon chopped fresh parsley
    1 cup beef stock*

Cut a pocket about an inch from the top of the ham, making incision from a side. Salt and pepper the ham outside and inside pocket as best you can. Combine raw apple slices, prunes, onions and parsley and then fill the pocket. Close the pocket with tooth picks. Place ham in a roasting pan with a cover and roast at 350° for 1¾ hours. Baste from time to time. Pour off excess fat. Remove roast to a warm platter and place roaster over a burner—add beef stock and deglaze by scraping bits off bottom of pan. Continue to cook and reduce by half the original volume. Remove toothpicks and slice part of the roast to expose filling. Pour gravy over and serve.

Suggested Wine: A chilled Tavel from the Côte du Rhône of France. Light as air rosé—refreshing and bright.

Poulet Provencal (Roast Chicken)

Serves 4

    1 2½- to 3-pound chicken
      Salt and freshly milled pepper
    2 tablespoons butter, softened
    6 tablespoons olive oil
  4-6 cloves of fresh garlic, peeled and halved
      Generous pinch each of rosemary, basil &
      thyme
    2 bay leaves
    1 medium cooking onion, chopped
    ½ cup dry red wine

Rub the cavity of the chicken with the softened butter, salt and fresh pepper. Heat the olive oil in a sauce pan slightly larger than the chicken and add the halved cloves of garlic and chopped onion. Sauté for a few minutes, then place the chicken in the pot, turn over several times to coat with the olive oil. Sprinkle with the salt and pepper and herbs. Continue to sauté the whole chicken, turning often, until it is browned nicely on all sides. Add the red wine and bay leaves, cover and simmer for about 30 minutes or until tender. Remove from the pot, cut into serving pieces and serve (hot or cold).

Suggested Wine: A dry red Bourdeaux wine: St. Emillion

Rumanian Duckling with Fresh Peas

Serves 4

     1 2 to 3-pound duckling, cut up
       A dash of salt
     2 tablespoons butter
     ½ cup water (or as needed)
     2 tablespoons diced raw bacon
 10-12 small onions, peeled and left whole
     1 pound fresh peas or 2 packages (10-ounce)
       frozen peas

Sprinkle duckling with salt to taste and sauté uncovered in butter slowly for an hour or until tender . . . add water as needed. Add bacon, onions and peas—cover and simmer until vegetables are tender (about 15-20 minutes). Remove to warm platter and serve.

Suggested Wines: A Cabernet Sauvignon from Bulgaria or Portugese Rosé, olé!

Zesty Roast Cornish Hens
Serves 4

8 strips of fatty bacon, cut in half
4 1-pound Cornish hens, trussed
  Juice of ½ lemon
  Grated rind of ½ lemon
½ pound whole butter
2½ pounds white seedless grapes
  Salt and freshly milled pepper to taste
2 cups dry white wine
2 teaspoons thyme and ½ cup freshly chopped parsley
½ teaspoon chopped grated onion

Rinse the cavity of each hen with cold water followed by a little lemon juice. Using a heavy dutch oven or 4-quart pot, melt butter over low heat. When melted, add half of bacon. Place all 4 hens on bacon and brown slowly (about 8-10 minutes per side). Remove the hens from the pot and loosely stuff with the grapes and replace in pot, breast up. Cover each hen with remaining bacon (2 pieces per hen). Add onion, thyme, parsley, salt and pepper and pour the wine over all. Sprinkle the hens with remaining grapes and lemon rind. Cover tightly and place in 400 degree oven to roast for 50 minutes to 1 hour.

Serve on a nicely garnished warm platter.

Suggested Wine: A New York State Rosé somewhat shallow and a hint on the sweet side.

Lemon Turkey Barbecue
Serves 6-7

1 6-7 pound turkey, thawed and cut up
¼ cup cooking oil
¼ cup soy sauce
1 large onion, peeled and chopped fine
1 teaspoon each—sugar, ground ginger (or fresh) and ground turmeric
½ teaspoon lemon peel, grated
3-4 tablespoons fresh lemon juice

Combine everything in a strong plastic bag and secure the opening so as not to leak. Marinate the turkey pieces overnight. Drain and reserve the marinade. Bake turkey in a 350° oven for 1 hour, basting occasionally with marinade. Turn oven to 450° for 15 minutes more cooking to brown well. Remove to warm platter and serve.

Breast of Chicken Veronique

Serves 4

- 4 ½-pound boneless breasts of chicken
- 2 cups of flour
- ½ cup oil and ½ cup butter
- 1 bay leaf
- 8 slices of fresh carrot
- 4 thin slices of onion
- 10 small pieces of fresh celery (a sprig of celery leaf will do)
- 8 additional teaspoons of flour
- 2 half pints of Half and Half
- Almost 2 cups of dry white wine
- Salt and freshly milled pepper to taste
- ½ pound of white seedless grapes

Dredge the breasts of chicken through the flour and season with salt and pepper. Melt the butter in a heavy sauté pan and add the oil; sauté the chicken breasts until lightly browned on all sides, about 6-10 minutes. Remove from the pan, then add to the drippings, bay leaf, carrot, sliced onion and celery. Simmer these for a few minutes, maybe 5, and add a few drops of water to deglaze the pan. Add the 8 teaspoons of flour to the vegetable mixture and stir into a smooth paste (roux). Add the Half and Half all at once and stir constantly until you have a smooth sauce. Remove from heat and add the wine and stir into the sauce. Strain and return to the skillet. Replace breasts in the sauce and gently simmer until chicken has been reheated thoroughly. Remove to an appropriate serving platter and garnish with seedless grapes.

Suggested Wine: A New York State dry white wine

NgOrongoro (Chicken with Peanuts) (A Congolese feast meal)

Serves 5-6

1 whole chicken 3-3½ pounds, cut up and dry
  Peanut oil
¼ pound bleached and roasted peanuts (crunchy
  peanut butter can substitute)
  Salt and freshly milled pepper to taste
1 teaspoon Cayenne pepper (Careful! It's really
  hot.)

Brown chicken pieces on all sides in a heavy skillet in about 5 tablespoons peanut oil (vegetable oil is fine but you will lack some flavor if used).

Crush peanuts in a mortar then heat in a few tablespoons water, creating a cream-like paste, or use ¼ cup crunchy peanut butter and water down slightly for the same paste-like texture. Pour the peanut paste over the chicken, add seasonings and simmer for about 30-45 minutes or until very tender. Lift out onto a serving platter and pour peanut sauce over and serve hot.

Chicken Burgundy

Serves 6

Preheat oven to 400°

1 4-pound roasting chicken
½ cup butter at room temperature
½ teaspoon dry mustard
½ teaspoon powdered ginger (or ½ teaspoon
  fresh chopped ginger)
3 cloves fresh garlic, crushed and minced
½ cup dry coarse bread crumbs
  About a pound of fresh mushrooms, halved
1 cup Burgundy wine (or dry red wine)
  Salt and freshly milled pepper

Salt the whole chicken inside and out and sprinkle with fresh pepper. Mix the garlic, mustard and ginger together with the soft butter, creating a paste and rub the chicken with the paste. Tie the legs and fold the wings of the chicken and roast uncovered in the hot oven for an hour, adding the mushrooms and wine at the halfway point. Baste often to keep moist so the flavor of the elegant wine permeates the chicken. When nicely browned, remove to an appropriate platter and serve with steamed fluffy white (buttered) rice and green vegetable.

Suggested Wine: Deep-flavored Red Burgundy (N.Y. State).

Sautéed Chicken with Orange and Grape Sauce

Serves 4-6

      1 4-pound fryer, cut up
        Flour
        Salt and freshly milled pepper to taste
        Oil to fry in
      3 tablespoons honey
      2 tablespoons fresh parsley
    3-4 tablespoons grated fresh orange rind
    1½ cups of seedless white grapes, halved
     ½ cup dry white wine
     ⅜ cup concentrated orange juice

Combine flour, salt and fresh pepper and coat chicken pieces. Heat oil in a heavy fry pan and brown chicken evenly on all sides. Add honey, orange juice, wine, orange rind, parsley, and mill a little fresh pepper over all. Cover and simmer for 10-15 minutes. Remove chicken to warm platter. Add grapes to fry pan and heat through. Pour sauce over chicken and serve piping hot.

Suggested Wine: Vouvray from the Loire Valley of France.

Braised Duck with Red Wine (Poland)

Serves 4

      1 duckling (about 4 pounds), cut up
        Salt
      2 cloves fresh garlic, peeled and crushed
      2 tablespoons butter
      2 tablespoons flour
      1 cup dry red wine
        Juice of 1 fresh lemon
      1 tablespoon lemon zest
        Generous pinch of sugar

Rub the pieces of duck with salt and crushed garlic and let stand for 2 hours. Brown the duck in hot butter. In a separate fry pan, brown flour, stirring constantly as not to allow sticking or burning. Add wine a little at a time, stirring with a wire whisk to prevent lumps. Add browned duck pieces and simmer for 1½ hours until meat is very tender. At the end of 1 hour, add the lemon rind and juice and the sugar. Remove to appropriate dish and serve.

Suggested Wine: California Zinfandel.

Pōōri Dada (Chicken stew from Biafrian Nigeria, S. West Africa)

Serves 6

- 1 stewing chicken 4-5 pounds cut up in stew-size portions
- 1 small can tomato paste
- 3 pounds peeled and grated onions
- 3 tablespoons ground thyme
- Cayenne pepper to taste for hot flavor
- ¼ cup peanut oil

NOTE: If a good sweat does not occur during the meal you have not used enough Cayenne pepper!!

In a heavy stew pot fry the chicken in the oil. Brown on all sides, add the onion and continue to cook until the onions begin to brown. Add the tomato paste and water as per directions on the paste can (usually two water to one can paste) and stir to blend smooth. Add thyme and cayenne pepper and simmer until chicken is tender and almost falling off the bone. (This insures the total integration of all spices.)

You serve this chicken dish either over white rice or with the special doughy bread called Khamom.

Khamōm (Doughy bread made on special holidays in Nigeria)

Serves 6 with stew

- 1 box Bisquick
- Hot water as per directions on the box

Heat the water and stir in the Bisquick flour and mix until all is blended, and continue to cook for about 5-7 minutes over low heat. The bread will resemble uncooked dough and will be sticky.

To serve, pull a 'hunk' off the dough ball and serve at the side of a good meat stew, usually chicken, eating a forkful of bread paste and forkful of stew in the same mouthful. This bread has a taming effect on Pōōri Dada.

Breast of Turkey Simmered with Leeks and Vegetables

Serves 6

2 leeks
½ head of green cabbage or iceberg lettuce (about 1 pound)
1 whole breast of turkey, uncooked, about 3 pounds
2 quarts (8 cups) chicken stock (or use rich canned chicken broth)*
1 teaspoon ginger (fresh or ground)
1 teaspoon salt
½ teaspoon peppercorns, freshly cracked
1 cup dry white wine
SAUCE:
2 tablespoons butter
3 tablespoons flour
2 cups stock in which turkey cooked
1 tablespoon prepared mustard
1 tablespoon mayonnaise
2 tablespoons fine bread crumbs

Trim the leeks, leaving an inch or two of the crisp green part, and spread the leaves. Place the leeks in a deep saucepan, add the cabbage, the breast of turkey, the chicken stock, the ginger, salt, cracked peppercorns, and wine. Cover the saucepan tightly (or use foil) and simmer for 1 hour. Preheat oven to 300°. Lift out the turkey breast, cabbage and leeks. Cut the turkey into thin slices; cut the cabbage and leeks into serving pieces. Place vegetables on an ovenproof serving platter. Cover the vegetables with sliced turkey and keep warm in a low oven. To prepare the sauce, melt the butter in a saucepan, stir in the flour to make a smooth paste. Gradually pour in 2 cups of turkey stock and stir until smooth. Add the mustard and mayonnaise. Remove the turkey and vegetables from the oven, then raise temperature to 400°. Pour sauce over turkey and sprinkle with bread crumbs. Return turkey to the oven and bake (400°) for 7 to 10 minutes or until the top is lightly colored.

Royal Chicken Paprika
Serves 4

⅓ cup butter
3 medium onions, peeled and sliced
2 cloves of fresh garlic, peeled and sliced thin
2 cups sliced fresh mushrooms
1 3-pound chicken cut up
2 cups water
   Salt and fresh milled pepper
1 tablespoon flour
1 teaspoon paprika
1 cup sour cream
6 tablespoons dry white wine

Melt the butter in a large heavy skillet and brown the chicken. Add the onion, garlic and fry for a few minutes longer—vegetables just turning brown . . . add the mushrooms and heat through. Add the water, salt and fresh pepper, cover and simmer for 30 minutes or until chicken is tender. Blend the flour and paprika into the sour cream and add to the pot. Mix thoroughly. Simmer for 5 minutes uncovered, add wine and stir in the sauce; bring to a light boil and cook 3 minutes more. Remove to a heated serving dish and dust with freshly snipped parsley garnish. Serve.

Suggested Wine: Côte du Phône, young and exciting.

Steamed Chicken with Ginger Root
Serves 2

1 broiler—split (2½ pounds)
   Pinch of salt
4 green onions, cut into 1-inch pieces end to end
¼ cup fresh ginger root, sliced thin (don't bother peeling)
⅓ cup dry sherry
1 tablespoon soy sauce

Place chicken halves on a rack in a heavy skillet or Dutch oven (with cover) and sprinkle with salt. Arrange onions and sliced ginger root around and on top. Combine wine and soy and pour over chicken and vegetables. Cover and steam, simmering over moderate heat for 45 minutes or until tender.

Suggested Wine: Warm sake or dry sherry wine.

Balinese Boiled Chicken

Serves 4

1-2½ to 3 pound chicken
- 1 quart of lightly salted (¼ teaspoon) water
- 1 celery stalk with leaves left whole
- 1 bay leaf
- 1 medium onion, peeled and studded with 2-4 cloves spikes
- 1 carrot, whole and unpeeled
- 1 teaspoon sugar
- 2 tablespoons butter
- 2 tablespoons cider vinegar
- 1 onion, peeled and chopped fine
- 2 tablespoons flour
- Pinch of ground cinnamon
- Pinch of ground mace
- Dash of salt
- 2 cups of hot chicken stock*
- ½ cup heavy cream at room temperature

Place the chicken in a large pot and cover with the cold quart of salted water. Add celery, bay leaf, onion with cloves, carrot and bring to a boil and simmer until chicken is tender. While the chicken is cooking, melt the butter in a skillet and cook chopped onion over moderate heat. Add the sugar, dissolve and then add vinegar. Reduce until vinegar has almost evaporated and sprinkle with flour. Stir to make roux, adding cinnamon, mace and season with salt. Gradually add the hot chicken stock and stir with a wire whisk until sauce thickens. Add room temperature cream and stir until completely integrated. Do not boil sauce. When chicken is done, strain broth and add half to the spice-cream sauce and blend until smooth. Cut chicken up and place on a heated platter. Pour cream-spice sauce over and serve.

Suggested Wine: Saint-Amour—a Beaujolais very light and full of fruit possessing a delightful richness.

Chicken and Clams, Valencia

Serves 4

- 3 pounds of boneless chicken breast cut into strips
  Salt and freshly milled pepper to taste
  Cooking oil
- 3 tablespoons butter
- 1 medium onion finely chopped
- 1 large green pepper diced
- 1 clove of fresh garlic, crushed and minced finely
- 1 bay leaf
- ¼ teaspoon saffron (optional)
- ¼ cup dry white wine
- 1 cup white rice
- 12 ounces (approx) chopped clams in juice (1 large can)

Sprinkle the chicken with salt and fresh pepper and fry in a heavy skillet with about ¼" of cooking oil in it until lightly browned on all sides. Remove chicken from pan and set aside. Pour off oil and add butter. When melted over moderate heat, add the green pepper, onion, garlic and bay leaf. Sauté slowly until the onions turn a slight bit yellow . . . now return the chicken to the pot and sprinkle the saffron over and pour in the wine.

Drain the clams and reserve the juice adding enough water to make 2½ cups liquid. Pour this liquid into a large enough saucepan to accommodate 3½ cups cooked rice . . . to the liquid in the pot, add a dash of salt and bring slowly to a boil, add your rice, stir and cover, lower heat to simmer and cook rice until done. When rice is cooked, add the clams and heat just enough to warm clams through. Spoon the rice and clam mixture onto a warm serving platter and place the chicken mixture on top of the rice . . . serve hot.

Suggested Wine: California "French" Colombard, a high-acid dry white wine.

Moroccan Couscous

Serves 6

- 1 medium eggplant
- 4 medium onions
- 1½ lean chicken meat, boned and cut for stew
- 1 small head cabbage, coarsely chopped
- ½ cup butter
- 1 teaspoon coriander
- 1 teaspoon saffron (optional)
- Freshly ground pepper and salt to taste
- 4 medium carrots, peeled
- 3 large tomatoes, cut for stew
- 1 sweet pepper, cut into strips
- 2 cups couscous
- 2 cups chicken stock*
- 1 cup raisins

Peel the eggplant and cut for stew. Peel and chop 2 onions. Combine onions, cabbage with chicken meat and toss. Melt 3 teaspoons butter in large pot and stir fry onions, cabbage and chicken mixture for 5 minutes. Add enough water to cover, plus remaining butter, stir in the spices, salt and pepper and bring to a boil. Cover and simmer 20 minutes. Quarter the remaining onions and carrots and add with tomatoes and pepper strips and eggplant to chicken. Simmer till vegetables are tender but not over-cooked.

Drain off most of the liquid and reserve. Keep stew warm!!

Place couscous into a saucepan large enough to hold and stir in 1 cup of reserved liquid and chicken stock and a dash of salt and some butter. Bring to a boil and turn to low and cook till all liquid is absorbed. When done, fluff with a fork and transfer to shallow platter.

Strain 1 cup of reserved liquid and pour over raisins in a small saucepan and cover. Over low heat, simmer about 5 minutes until raisins are plump and tender.

Transfer hot stew to platter and serve couscous and raisin sauce on the side.

Chicken with Olives
Serves 4

2½ pounds chickens, cut into serving pieces
3 tablespoons olive oil
2 onions, finely chopped
2 cloves garlic, crushed
2 tablespoons flour
½ cup white wine
¼ cup white vermouth
½ cup chicken broth*
1 tablespoon tomato paste
2 tomatoes, peeled, and chopped
    Salt, freshly milled pepper
1 bay leaf
½ teaspoon marjoram
8 green olives, pitted
8 black olives, pitted

Brown chicken in hot oil and transfer to a casserole. Sauté onions and garlic in the same oil. Stir in the flour and add the wine, vermouth, and chicken broth. Add tomato paste and tomatoes. Season with salt and pepper, add marjoram and bay leaf. Cover and cook in a 350° oven for 30 minutes. Garnish with black and green olives.

Suggested Wine: Boca—a red from Northern Italy

Roast Chicken India
Serves 4-6

1 3-pound frying chicken
½ teaspoon ground ginger
    Dash coriander
    Dash cayenne pepper
¾ cup grated fresh onion
⅜ cup melted butter
½ teaspoon turmeric
    Salt to taste
¼ cup plain yogurt
¼ cup light cream (Half & Half)
1 medium onion, peeled and sliced into thin rings

Combine ginger, coriander and cayenne pepper and rub the chicken inside and out. Place in a roasting pan. Combine grated onion, melted butter, turmeric, salt, yogurt, and Half & Half and pour half this mixture over chicken. Roast at 350° for 1 hour, basting with remaining onion-yogurt mixture from time to time. After the hour, arrange sliced onions atop the chicken and roast an additional 40 minutes or until tender. Remove to an appropriate platter, pour sauce over and serve.

Roast Chicken Izmir with Apricots

Serves 4

- 4 tablespoons butter
- 6 tablespoons honey
- 1 tablespoon rose water
  Salt and freshly milled pepper to taste
- 4-5 pound roasting chicken
- 1 pound fresh apricots, halved and pitted (or 1 large can whole apricots, drained and pits removed)
- 1 tablespoon sugar
- ½ cup sliced almonds or chopped pistachios, toasted

Combine butter, 4 tablespoons honey, rose water, salt and fresh pepper and rub the chicken inside and out. Place in a roasting pan and sear in 425° oven, turning chicken to brown evenly and seal in juices. Lower heat to 350° and add the apricots, remaining honey and sugar to the pan juices. Stir to blend juices and new additions. Roast, basting often to glaze, for 1 hour or until chicken is tender. Remove chicken to a heated platter. Spoon juices and apricots over and sprinkle with nuts and serve.

Suggested Wine: California Fumé Blanc.

Honey Glazed Cornish Hens

Serves 4

- Open 4-quart casserole (stove to table variety)
- 4 16-ounce Cornish hens
- 1 pound sliced bacon
- ¼ cup butter
- ¼ cup honey
  Salt and freshly milled pepper
  Cognac or brandy

Rinse hens under cold water and dry as best you can. Wrap or "lard" each hen with a few strips of raw bacon and place in casserole, breast up. In a small saucepan, slowly melt butter, adding honey. Pour the butter and honey mixture over hens coating them nicely and roast (open) in a 400° oven for approximately 1 hour. Check for doneness.

When ready to serve, remove to table and pour cognac over all and ignite. A wonderfully simple but elegant meal.

Suggested Wine: Marqués de Riseal—a light dry red wine of Spain.

Cornish Game Hens Provencale

Serves 4

- 4 16-ounce Cornish hens
  Butter
- 1 medium onion, peeled and sliced
- 1 medium carrot, peeled and sliced
- 3 tender stalks of celery, sliced
- 2 ounces dry sherry wine
- 3 tablespoons flour
- 2 cups veal stock or beef stock
- 4 ounces Madeira wine
  3-4 tablespoons red currant jelly
- 4 ounces dry red wine
  Juice of ½ lemon
- 8 ounces seedless white grapes
- ¼ cup chopped parsley
  Salt and freshly milled pepper to taste

Melt butter enough to cover the bottom of a heavy skillet and over high heat sauté carrot, onion, and celery. When carrots turn a bright orange and soften a little, lower heat to medium high and place hens on bed of sautéed vegetables. Add sherry wine. Season generously with salt and pepper and continue to fry on all sides.

Place pan with hens and vegetables in 375° oven and roast 45 minutes.

Make a roux with 3 tablespoons flour and 3 tablespoons butter in a shallow pot. Gradually stir in Madeira wine, veal stock and currant jelly and bring to a boil. Add red wine and lemon juice and stir. Cook until thickened. Carefully remove hens to serving platter and keep warm. Place roasting pan on top of range and stir sauce into cooked vegetables and simmer for 5 minutes. Sieve into a clean pan and discard vegetables. Sprinkle hens with white grapes and dust with parsley. Serve with Madeira sauce on the side.

Suggested Wine: A red wine from Provence.

Julienne of Turkey with Hearts of Palm Bake

Serves 6

- 6 large slices of cooked turkey breast, cut into julienne strips
- 3 hard boiled eggs, sliced
- 1 can hearts of palm, drained and cross-cut into slices
- 3 tablespoons chopped fresh chive
- 4 tablespoons butter
- 4 tablespoons flour
- 1 cup rich chicken stock (reduced from 2 cups)*
- 1 cup Half and Half at room temperature
  Salt and freshly milled pepper to taste
  Pinch of paprika
- 1 small jar pimientos in oil, drained and sliced
- ¾ cup coarse bread crumbs
- 2 tablespoons butter

Arrange julienned turkey breast, hearts of palm slices and sliced egg in a shallow buttered baking dish. Melt butter in a small skillet and fry chopped chive until butter takes on a green tint. Add flour and stir to make a roux. Gradually add stock and Half and Half, stirring constantly with wire whisk until sauce is thickened (slightly green colored sauce). Season with salt and fresh pepper. Pour sauce over turkey and hearts of palm casserole. Sprinkle with bread crumbs. Color top with paprika and dot with butter and pimientos. Place casserole in a preheated 350° oven and bake open for 15 minutes or until heated through. Serve in casserole.

Suggested Wine: Johannisberg Riesling.

Breast of Chicken Siena with Orange-Raisin Sauce

Serves 4

    4 whole breasts of chicken, boned and halved
      (4 ounces each)
¼ pound butter
    3 tablespoons flour
      Generous pinch of paprika
      Salt and freshly milled pepper to taste
    1 pint Half and Half at room temperature
½ cup raisins
½ cup fresh orange juice
      Parsley bouquets for garnish

Soak raisins in orange juice. Meanwhile, brown the chicken breasts in butter in a heavy skillet. Lower heat and simmer for 20 minutes covered. Remove chicken to platter and keep warm. Pour off all but about 3 tablespoons butter and pan juices. Stir in flour to make roux—add paprika, salt and fresh pepper. Add Half and Half and cook, stirring constantly (scrape bottom, deglaze pan) until sauce has thickened. Pour in orange-raisin mixture and heat; pour over chicken and serve.

Suggested Wine: Almadén Gamay—a "happy wine."

Persian Lamb Stew

Serves 6

    3 medium onions, peeled and chopped finely
    4 tablespoons butter
    3 pounds of lamb for stew (lean)
    2 cups dried apricots
    1 cup seedless raisins
½ cup chicken stock*
      Juice of ½ fresh lemon
½ cup prune juice
    3 tablespoons apricot preserve

Melt butter in a heavy skillet and fry onions until just tender. Push aside and sauté lamb meat until browned evenly. Add dry apricots and raisins and simmer 5-8 minutes to blend flavors—add additional butter if needed (you must keep an eye out for drying). Pour in chicken stock—stir well and cover. Simmer, adding more stock if needed, for 2 hours. Sauce should be very thick and sweet. In the last half hour of cooking, add the lemon and prune juices and apricot preserve. Remove stew to deep heated platter and serve.

Lamb Pilau

Serves 6-10

2¼ pounds boned and cubed loin of lamb
    Butter as needed
  3 onions, finely chopped
  2 cloves of garlic, chopped
  1 stick cinnamon
  1 tablespoon cardamom
  6 cloves
  1 level teaspoon finely chopped fresh ginger
    (½ teaspoon ground)
 ½ pound rice cooked in chicken stock
  4 ounces blanched almonds

Boil the meat until tender. Lightly fry the onions and garlic in the butter. Add the spices and continue frying for 4 minutes while stirring. Stir in the rice and add the chicken bouillon, which should cover it well. If there is not sufficient bouillon, add boiling water. Season with salt, cover the pan and simmer until the water is absorbed and the rice cooked. Now add the cubes of meat and toss in the almonds which have been lightly fried in butter. Remove to serving platter and garnish with additional fried sliced onions.

Beef Liver with Tomato Sauce—Greek Style

Serves 4

  4 slices of baby beef liver, 6 ounces each
 ¼ cup butter
 ½ cup white wine
  1 clove garlic, peeled and crushed
  1 tablespoon tomato paste—dilute with ¾ cup
    water
  1 small onion, peeled and minced finely
  2 tablespoons chopped fresh parsley
    Salt and freshly milled pepper to taste

Cut the liver slices into strips (1 inch wide). Rinse under cold water and drain well. Heat the butter in a heavy fry pan and lightly sauté the onion and garlic 2 minutes, add liver strips; sauté browning well. Add the wine—bring to a boil. Add the tomato paste dilute, parsley, season with salt and fresh pepper to taste and let simmer uncovered until the sauce is reduced to half and is thick and fragrant. Remove to a warm platter and serve.

Suggested Wine: Mauro Romeiko from the Isle of Crete.

Finland's Chopped Beef Liver Hash

Serves 4

    1 pound baby beef liver, parboiled and minced
3-4 cups whole milk
    1 cup rice (converted)
    1 medium onion, peeled and chopped
    2 tablespoons butter
    3 tablespoons light Karo syrup
    ⅔ cup raisins
      Salt and freshly milled pepper to taste
      A pinch of marjoram

Pour rice and cold milk into a saucepan and cook rice until tender (25 minutes). Let the rice cool. Preheat oven to 375°. Sauté onion in half the butter until soft and transparent. Combine the chopped liver, onions, syrup, raisins and season with marjoram, salt and fresh pepper. Gently stir to mix meat and spices through rice. Spoon into a buttered casserole and bake for 1 hour. Serve with cranberry jelly.

Suggested Beverage: Beer.

Hungarian Chicken Stew

Serves 6
Is Served Over Wide Noodles

    1 large green pepper
    ½ cup chopped onions
    ½ cup fresh mushrooms
    2 sweet dill pickles
    1 tablespoon Hungarian paprika
    1 3-pound chicken, cut up
    ½ cup oil
      Salt and fresh pepper to taste
    ½ c. bottled ketchup
      Fresh string beans (optional)
      Fresh parsley, chopped

Halve and seed the pepper, dice; slice the pickles and mushrooms and rub the chicken with the paprika. Fry the chicken in a heavy skillet until brown on all sides and add the peppers. Boil the green beans until almost done but not tender. Remove the chicken and add the onions and mushrooms, pickles and green beans to the pan and simmer for about 5 minutes or until beans are tender. Add the ketchup and bring to a boil and remove from heat. Season with salt and pepper. Arrange chicken on a platter of cooked wide noodles and spoon the sauce and vegetables over chicken and noodles and sprinkle with fresh parsley. Serve hot.

Stewed Chicken Legs with Mushrooms

Serves 4

    2 pounds of chicken legs (no thighs)
    6 tablespoons butter
    1 pound of mushrooms, wiped clean and sliced
    2 or 3 cloves of fresh garlic, peeled and crushed
    1 small onion, peeled and sliced
    1 celery stalk, chopped with leaves
      Salt and freshly milled pepper to taste
    3 tablespoons dry gin
    2 tablespoons flour
    ½ cup of milk, heated
    ½ cup chicken stock*
    ¼ cup heavy cream at room temperature
      Freshly chopped parsley for garnish

Melt the butter in a heavy skillet and sauté garlic and chicken legs until legs are browned on all sides. Remove both garlic and chicken. Add the onion and celery to fry pan and cook until tender. Replace only chicken legs and season with salt and fresh pepper. Sprinkle with the gin and cook until gin has evaporated. Sprinkle the meat mixture with flour and stir with a wooden spoon gently as you add heated milk and stock. Cover the pan and simmer over very low heat for 30 minutes or until chicken is tender. Add heavy cream and stir to blend into sauce—cover and cook 5 minutes more. Add sliced mushrooms and cook open 5 minutes to heat and wilt mushrooms. Dust with chopped fresh parsley. Remove to warm platter and serve.

Suggested Wine: Barbera d'Alba—young and exciting from northern Italy.

Mushroom-Chicken Newburg

Serves 4

    3 egg yolks, slightly beaten
    1 cup light cream
    ½ teaspoon salt and freshly milled pepper to
      taste
    ½ teaspoon ground marjoram
    2 cups cooked chicken cut in small pieces
    1 cup sliced fresh mushrooms
    3 tablespoons butter
    ¼ cup sherry
    2 tablespoons brandy
    4 slices toast or patty shells
      Paprika

Mushroom-Chicken Newburg
(continued)

Combine yolks and half the cream. Mix salt, pepper and marjoram to paste with a little of the cream mixture. Add to cream and cook in top of double boiler until custard consistency, stirring constantly. Sauté chicken and mushrooms in butter gently for about 5 minutes or until heated through. Remove from heat and stir in liquor. Combine sauce and chicken and blend well. Serve immediately on pieces of toast or in patty shells. Garnish with paprika.

Suggested Wine: St. Emillian or a Big Bordeaux red wine.

Persian Spinach and Lamb Dolma
Serves 4

    1 pound ground lean lamb
    1 medium onion, peeled and minced
    2 cloves fresh garlic, peeled, crushed and
      minced
      Salt and freshly milled pepper to taste
      Pinch of cayenne pepper
    1 pound fresh leaf spinach—stems removed,
      washed and dried
      Olive oil
      Juice of ½ lemon
    2 medium tomatoes, peeled and chopped

In a large bowl, knead lamb, onion and garlic together for 5 minutes to assure a smooth, blended mixture. Season (about halfway through) with salt, fresh pepper and cayenne. Using a teaspoon, portion lamb mixture into palms of hand and shape into small meatballs.

Have a pot of boiling water ready. Plunge spinach leaves into the pot just long enough to soften them and bring out alive green color. Using 2 leaves, wrap the lamp meatballs, tucking leaves to envelope meat. Heat olive oil in a Dutch oven (with cover) and place the spinach rolls in packed closely, but not too tight. Squeeze lemon juice over all. Add tomatoes and place plate upside down on rolls to prevent their floating. Cover pan and simmer on lowest possible heat 1-1½ hours. Carefully remove to an appropriate serving platter. Garnish with lemon wedges and serve. Wonderful hors d'oeuvres, too!

Elegant Roast Chicken à la Beira

Serves 4

- 1 3-pound chicken
- 8 slices Canadian bacon
- 1 cup cottage cheese
  Salt and freshly milled pepper to taste
- 2 tablespoons butter
- 2 tablespoons olive oil
- 8 small potatoes, peeled and halved
- 8 small onions, peeled
- 4 strips of bacon

Start at the neck end of chicken and run your fingers under the skin (breast side only) to loosen meat. Slip the slices of Canadian bacon under skin, one at a time, making sure the slices are flat and smooth. Fill the cavity of the chicken with the cottage cheese and secure legs with string. Season the chicken with salt and fresh pepper. Place the chicken, breast up, in a baking dish (suitable for table service). Rub the surface with butter and oil and surround with potatoes and onions. Lard the breast (cover with bacon strips) and roast open at 350° for about 1 hour—or until chicken is tender. Untie legs and serve at the table. Do not carve—cut into quarters and serve cottage cheese like stuffing.

Suggested Wine: A rich, fragrant Pomerol.

Calf's Liver Sauté with Curried Onions

Serves 4

- 1 large sweet onion, peeled and sliced thin
- ¼ cup dry sherry wine
- ½ teaspoon curry powder
  Salt and freshly ground pepper
- ¼ cup white raisins
- 2 teaspoons butter
- 1 pound calf's liver, sliced thin

In a heavy skillet simmer the onion slices in the sherry wine until tender and the wine is absorbed—maybe 8-10 minutes. Add the curry, salt, fresh pepper, raisins and butter and continue to cook. Push the onion-curry mixture aside and place the liver slices into pan and fry to your desired degree of doneness, turning only once. Remove to a warm platter and smother with the curried onions.

Breast of Chicken All'Antinore
Serves 4

Seasoned flour (salt, pepper and granulated garlic)
4 8-ounce boneless chicken breasts
3 tablespoons whole butter
2 tablespoons olive oil
1 #2 can artichoke hearts, drained
12 large white mushroom caps
½ cup Marsala wine
Chopped fresh parsley

Dredge each chicken breast through seasoned flour (tap off excess). Using a heavy fry pan, melt butter with olive oil over moderate heat (medium high setting) and sauté breasts until nicely browned on both sides. Add artichoke hearts and mushroom caps and continue to cook until mushroom caps are hot through. Drain off ½ the liquid and oil from pan and add the Marsala wine. It will flare once, be careful. Gently move the pan back and forth over heat for a moment or two. Remove chicken breasts to a warm platter, pour sauce over, and dust with parsley.

Suggested Wine: A young white Bordeaux, Blanc de Blanc.

Calf's Liver in Heaven and Earth (Germany)
Serves 4

4 slices of calf's liver, floured and fried (keep hot)
2 teaspoons grated lemon zest
2½ cups chunky applesauce (homemade is best)
2 cups mashed fresh potatoes
½ pound sliced bacon, diced
5 onions, peeled and sliced
Salt and freshly milled pepper to taste

Mix lemon zest and applesauce together, then fold into mashed potatoes. In a heavy fry pan, cook the diced bacon, adding sliced onions after the fat has begun to run in the pan. Cook until browned slightly. Stir ½ of onion mixture into hot potato mixture and season with salt and fresh pepper. Arrange half the sautéed onion-bacon mixture on platter, place hot slices of liver on top and spoon a generous dollop of potato-bacon mixture on top.

Suggested Wine: A cool Mosel-Saar-Ruwer district wine.

Julia's Russian Chicken with Walnut Sauce

Serves 4-6

- 1 large frying chicken, cut up
  Seasoned flour (salt and fresh pepper)
- 3 tablespoons oil
- 1 clove fresh garlic, lightly bruised
- 2 tablespoons butter
- 1 clove fresh garlic, peeled, crushed and minced
- ½ cup finely chopped walnuts
- 1 or 2 medium onions, peeled and chopped
- 1 tablespoon flour
- 1 cup chicken stock*
  Dash ground allspice
  Dash ground nutmeg
  Dash ground cinnamon
- 1 tablespoon cider vinegar
  Salt and freshly milled pepper to taste
  Chopped fresh parsley

Dredge chicken pieces in seasoned flour and set aside. In a heavy large skillet, sauté bruised garlic in oil until lightly brown. Discard garlic and sauté chicken pieces, turning to brown evenly. Lower heat, cover and simmer chicken for 30 minutes or until tender. Remove to heated platter and keep warm. Add butter to skillet—add minced garlic, walnuts and onion. Stir-fry until onion is soft and transparent. Sprinkle with flour and stir to blend—cook 2 minutes to make roux. Add stock, spices, vinegar and adjust seasoning (salt and fresh pepper). Cook, stirring until thickened. Pour sauce over chicken (save some for table service) and sprinkle with fresh parsley and serve.

Suggested Wine: Great Western's De Chaunac—a little harsh if young, but oh how romantically Russian!.

Paella (Chicken)
Serves 6

- 1 chicken cut up (approx. 2½ pounds)
  Olive oil (or vegetable oil)
- 2 large onions, peeled and chopped coarsely
- 4 cloves garlic, peeled, chopped finely
- 2-3 leaves from fresh celery stalks (optional, but good)
  Salt and freshly milled pepper to taste
- 3-4 pistils saffron, crushed and soaked in a little water (optional)
- ¼ pound spicy sausage (chorizo if available or beef sausage, Polish or German style)
- 2 cups chicken stock*
- 1½ cups converted rice, uncooked

Brown cut-up chicken in oil, using heavy skillet. Add onions, garlic, celery, sausage and seasonings and continue to fry until onions are soft. Transfer this mixture to a deep baking dish in which you already have 1½ cups uncooked rice. Stir well, making sure the oil and herbs are well blended with the rice. Add chicken stock and bake, uncovered for 40-50 minutes in a 400° oven (or until rice has absorbed all liquid and browned a little). Do not stir while cooking. Fluff before serving.

Lemon Lamb Chops
Serves 6

- 12 small lamb rib chops
- 4 tablespoons cooking oil
- ⅓ cup water
- ¼ cup lemon juice
- 1 tablespoon shredded lemon peel
- 24 thin slices of lemon
- 1 tablespoon Worcestershire sauce
  Salt and freshly milled pepper
  A pinch dry oregano
  A pinch dry rosemary
- 1 tablespoon cornstarch

In a large heavy skillet brown the chops in oil, about 12 minutes. Combine water, lemon juice, Worcestershire sauce, oregano, rosemary, salt and pepper, and pour over meat. Cover and simmer over low heat until tender (30 minutes). Remove chops to a warm serving platter and pour pan juices into a measuring cup, skimming off any fat. Add water enough to make a cup and return to skillet. Blend the cornstarch into cold water and add to simmering juices, stirring constantly. Add lemon peel and cook until thickened. Spoon some over meat and garnish with lemon slices—pass gravy at table.

Chicken Chinese with Sweet Peppers

Serves 4

   2 whole chicken breasts, boned
   1 clove garlic, peeled and crushed
   4 tablespoon olive oil
   3 tablespoons soy sauce
     Salt and freshly milled pepper to taste
   2 teaspoons cornstarch
   2 green sweet peppers
   1 red sweet pepper
   8 green onions
   3 celery stalks
   ¼ teaspoon sugar
   ¼ cup cold water

Cut chicken into 1-inch pieces. Combine chicken, garlic, 1 tablespoon of oil, 2 tablespoons of soy sauce, salt, pepper and 1 teaspoon of cornstarch in a mixing bowl and let stand for at least 30 minutes to marinate. Cut the peppers into 1-inch pieces, removing seeds and membrane. Cut onions and celery into ½-inch pieces. Heat the remaining 3 tablespoons of oil in a wok. Add the peppers and celery and stir-fry for 3 minutes. Add the onions and stir-fry 2 minutes. Remove the peppers and onions, using a slotted spoon. Keep warm. Place the chicken in the hot oil in the wok and stir-fry for 5 minutes. Combine the remaining 1 teaspoon of cornstarch, sugar and water and pour over the chicken. Add the vegetables and combine carefully, cooking over low heat for about 3 minutes. Remove to appropriate dish and serve.

Chicken Stew

Serves 6

  12 chicken thighs (whole chicken cut up will do)
     Salt and freshly milled black pepper
     Olive oil (vegetable will do—but not as well)
   2 tablespoons cognac
   1 large onion, diced
     1-2 cloves garlic, crushed and minced
   1 green pepper, cut in strips
   2 cups sliced mushrooms
   1 cup diced smoked ham
     Whole fresh tomatoes or 1 #3 can plum tomatoes
   1 cup white wine
   2 more tablespoons cognac
     1-2 tablespoons minced parsley

Chicken Stew (continued)

Sprinkle chicken with salt and pepper to taste. Sauté in oil until browned. Add cognac and set ablaze. (Careful!)

When flame goes out, add onion, green pepper, garlic, mushrooms and ham. Mash tomatoes (either fresh or canned) and add with wine to chicken. Cover, simmer for about an hour or until chicken is tender and well cooked. Add second tablespoon cognac and let simmer 10 minutes longer to integrate the brandy flavor. Carefully lift the chicken onto a warm serving platter and keep warm. Skim fat from remaining liquid and if the sauce seems too thin, boil hard to reduce. Spoon sauce over chicken and sprinkle parsley over all on warm platter—then serve.

Suggested Wine: A nice chilled Chianti from Italy!

Baked Lamb Chops Ala Navarra
Serves 4

    8 thin loin lamb chops (lean)
    2 tablespoons olive oil
    2 tablespoons butter
    ½ pound boiled ham, cubed
    1 large onion, peeled and chopped finely
    2 medium tomatoes, peeled and chopped
      Salt to taste
    1 teaspoon sugar

Combine oil and butter and melt in a heavy skillet. Fry the lamb chops until browned on both sides and remove. Sauté the ham cubes and onion in the same oil until onion is soft. Add the tomatoes and simmer for 10 minutes. Season with salt and sugar. Pour ham-onion-tomato mixture into a shallow casserole and place lamb chops on top of sauce. Cover and bake at 350° for 20 minutes or until lamb is tender. Remove from oven, uncover and serve in casserole.

Suggested Wine: Madiran Avigorour Red from Armagnac.

"Ladies' Thighs" or Lamb Köfte
Serves 4

- 1 pound chopped or coarsely ground lamb meat
- 3 ounces bel paese cheese
- ½ cup dry white wine
- ¼ cup Uncle Ben's converted rice
  Olive oil
- 1 small onion, peeled and minced finely
- 1 teaspoon crushed dry mint leaves
  Salt and freshly milled pepper to taste
- 1 clove garlic, crushed and minced finely
- 2 tablespoons butter
- 2 eggs, well beaten
  Fresh parsley bouquets for garnish

Coarse grate the cheese (shred). In a saucepan bring wine to a good boil. Add rice, cover and simmer until rice absorbs all the wine. In a heavy skillet, heat oil over low heat, add onion and garlic and sauté until soft and fragrant, but not browned. Add lamb meat to fry pan and stir-fry (breaking meat up as much as possible) until lightly browned. Remove contents of fry pan to a large mixing bowl. Add cheese, rice, mint, salt and fresh pepper. Knead the mixture for about 3 minutes (squeeze and push with hands until all ingredients blend). Shape oval cutlet of lamb about ¾ inch thick and 2 inches long.

Wipe out heavy skillet. Melt butter over moderate heat and add 1 tablespoon olive oil. Dip each lamb cutlet into egg and sauté until golden on both sides. Remove to warm platter, garnish with fresh parsley bouquets and serve.

Breast of Chicken Piccata
Serves 4

- 2 large chicken breasts, skin removed
- ¼ cup flour
  Salt and freshly milled pepper
  Paprika
- 3 tablespoons butter
- 2 tablespoons olive oil
- 2 cloves of fresh garlic, peeled, leave whole
- 4-6 tablespoons Marsala or Madeira wine (cream sherry will substitute)
  Juice of 1 fresh lemon
  Several thin slices of lemon
- 2 teaspoons capers
  Chopped parsley for garnish

Breast of Chicken Piccata (continued)

Pound the chicken breasts gently to very thin—cut in half (makes 4 pieces). Combine flour, salt, fresh pepper and paprika. Flour each piece of chicken breast, both sides.

Heat butter and oil in a heavy skillet and add whole garlic cloves. Place chicken in hot butter and sauté (do it twice as not to crowd chicken) until lightly browned on both sides. Remove and keep warm. Drain off most of butter-oil leaving only 2 tablespoons. (Remove and throw garlic away.) Pour wine into pan and deglaze (scrape the bottom to loosen any browned bits). Add lemon juice and slices. Return chicken to pan and shake back and forth until sauce thickens—add capers. Remove to serving platter. Sprinkle with parsley.

Suggested Wine: Gerwürztraminer.

Lamb Chops Sauté with Mushrooms
Serves 4

> 8 small (2-3 ounces each) thin lamb chops
> Flour
> 2 eggs, lightly beaten
> Butter
> ½ teaspoon each: leaf tarragon, leaf savory and leaf mint
> ½ cup finely chopped mushrooms
> Salt and freshly milled pepper
> 1 clove garlic, peeled and crushed
> 1 pound fresh mushrooms, sliced
> Juice of ½ fresh lemon

Flatten the lamb chops gently with the heel of your hand and lightly dredge through flour. Combine herbs with egg and dip each chop to coat. Dip into finely chopped mushrooms and pat gently to assure the mushrooms adhere to the chops. Melt butter in a heavy skillet and sauté the chops until nicely browned on both sides (4-5 minutes, each side) and remove to a warm platter. Add garlic and mushrooms to butter and sprinkle with lemon, salt and fresh pepper to taste. Sauté for 3 minutes. Arrange chops with bones out, leaving a circle in the center of serving platter. Place sautéed mushrooms in circle and serve.

Suggested Wine: Rosé, chilled.

Chicken Breasts on Rice and Walnuts
Serves 4

- 2 medium onions, peeled and chopped
- 2 firm medium tomatoes, peeled and chopped
- 1 leek, washed of all sand—sliced
- 3 tablespoons finely chopped fresh parsley
- 4 chicken breasts
- 1 cup long grain rice (converted and uncooked, preferred)
- ¼ cup vegetable oil
- ½ cup chopped walnuts (more if you like them)
- ¼ cup butter

Melt the butter in a heavy skillet and sauté the vegetables together for 5 minutes; add the chopped parsley to the vegetable mixture. Meanwhile, put on a pot of water for rice (two parts water to one part rice) salt a bit and cook rice until tender. Open the breast of chicken, lay flat on a chopping board and flatten with the side of a meat cleaver or gently with a meat mallet. Place a good tablespoon or more of the cooked vegetables on the flattened breast and fold to close (envelope style). Heat the oil in a heavy skillet and fry the chicken breasts over moderate heat for about 4 minutes on a side (careful not to burn). The chicken and rice should be cooked at about the same time. Rinse the rice in hot tap water to remove the starch and place as a foundation on a warm serving platter on which you arrange the stuffed breasts of chicken. Warm the walnuts (shelled) over high heat for a moment and sprinkle lavishly over all.

Suggested Wine: Rosé d'Anjou.

Braised Leg of Lamb Orensana
Serves 6

- 1 4-pound boneless leg of lamb (tied)
  Salt and freshly milled pepper to taste
- 1 tablespoon butter
- 2 tablespoons oil
- 3 carrots, peeled and quartered lengthwise
- 3 small onions, peeled and quartered
- 2 cups of veal or beef stock*
- 1 16-ounce can of lima beans, drained

Braised Leg of Lamb
Orensana (continued)

Season the leg of lamb with salt and fresh pepper. Combine oil and butter in a dutch oven (with cover) and brown on all sides. Remove the lamb and add carrots and onions and brown in the same oil. Pour off the fat and replace the lamb in the pot and add stock. Bring to a boil, reduce heat, cover and simmer for 2 hours or until lamb is tender. Add lima beans and cook another 15-20 minutes. Remove lamb to platter and let "rest" 10 minutes. Meanwhile, allow sauce to reduce. Slice lamb and remove vegetables from gravy and surround sliced lamb with vegetables. Spoon some gravy over slices to moisten and pour the rest into a gravy bowl. Serve with sauce on the side.

Suggested Wine: New York State Rosé—cool and refreshing with this lamb dish.

Chicken Roasted in Beer
Serves 4

2½ 3-pound chicken
　　Flour
　8 tablespoons butter
¼ cup olive oil
　2 large onions, peeled and sliced
　1 clove garlic, peeled and crushed
　　Salt and freshly milled pepper to taste
　2 cups of beer
　1 cup heavy cream

Roll chicken in flour to lightly coat. Heat the butter and oil in a deep heavy dutch oven and sauté the garlic, onion and chicken until the chicken has browned evenly all around (maybe 10 minutes frying). Place browned chicken in a shallow roaster and season with salt and fresh pepper to taste. Pour the beer in, cover and place in a preheated 400° oven for 50 minutes to an hour (check occasionally and baste with water if needed). When the chicken is done, remove to a heated platter. Place roaster over a stove top burner and deglaze by boiling the pan juices and rubbing the bits off the bottom with a wooden spoon (you may need a little water). Lower heat and add room temperature heavy cream and reduce for 5 minutes, stirring. Pour sauce over roasted chicken and serve. Don't carve into slices—quarter the chicken and serve in pieces.

Suggested Beverage: Beer, of course!

Coliva

(An ancient Roman recipe used at funeral celebrations rather than weddings. Here we offer the Rumanian version.)

½ pound whole wheat grain
2 cups water
1 cup sugar
½ teaspoon salt
4 tablespoons chopped walnut meat
A generous dash of ground cinnamon
Grated zest of 2 lemons

Combine all ingredients in a heavy saucepan and cook—simmering to a thick paste. Allow to cool completely and shape into a pyramid on an elegant serving dish. Dust with confectioners sugar and garnish with candied fruits and half walnuts.

Middle Eastern Lamb Meatballs with Dill Sauce

Serves 4

1 pound ground lamb
Salt and freshly ground pepper to taste
½ teaspoon ground coriander
¼ teaspoon ground cinnamon
1 medium onion, peeled and minced finely
½ fine bulgur (cracked wheat)
1 egg, well beaten
1 quart beef stock*
1 stick butter (¼ pound)
¼ cup flour
1 cup yogurt
1 tablespoon dry dill weed

Combine lamb with salt and fresh pepper, spices, onion, bulgur and egg. Mix very well. Shape small meatballs between palms of your hand. In a 2-quart saucepan, boil stock, add ½ the meatballs, cover and simmer 10 minutes. Remove meatballs from stock with slotted spoon and repeat with remaining lamb meatballs. Strain and measure out 1 pint broth. Keep broth hot.

In a second saucepan, melt butter, add flour and blend well to create a roux. Slowly add hot stock, stirring constantly with wire whisk. Return to moderate heat and continue to stir until sauce thickens. Add meatballs again and heat through. Remove from stove—add, stirring, yogurt and dill weed. Transfer to appropriate serving dish and serve.

Turkish Lamb Stew

Serves 4-6

  2 pounds lamb stew (beef will substitute)
    cubed to 1-inch squares
12 green onions (scallions) chopped coarsely
  1 large onion, chopped finely
  1 romaine lettuce, cut in small pieces
  1 teaspoon sugar
    Salt to taste
  ½ cup fresh chopped dill or ¼ cup dry dillweed
3½ tablespoons butter
    Fresh milled pepper, black (optional)
  ¾ tablespoon flour

Knead all ingredients except dill and flour. Place this lamb and vegetable mixture into a ceramic or heavy steel bowl which holds all nicely. Invert a large pot and place over bowl. Turn upside down (pot now in cooking position) without breaking the seal of the bowl against the pot's bottom!

Place a minimum of 4 pounds weight on bowl to insure pressure, turn heat to medium high until you see natural juices begin to fill around bowl, lower heat to low and stew for approximately 1-1½ hours. Remove pot from heat, blend the flour into ¾ cup cold water, add some of the au jus (natural juices from stew) to the flour and cook in a saucepan over low heat until coats spoon (stir constantly). Add dill to this sauce, bring to a boil and remove from heat. Returning to stew pot and without disturbing the bowl, pour off all liquid and reserve. Remove dome and serve meat on heated platter with the dill sauce over all.

Vegetables 111

How does your garden grow?

Vegetables, as I see them, fall neatly into categories. The plant itself is my key: roots, stem, leaf, flower, fruit and finally seeds. Mushrooms and truffles are fungi—and fungi are plants. Therefore, a vegetable!

A little forethought and we can all be better at vegetable cookery.

Root vegetables are best started cooking in cold water. As the water warms, so too the vegetables—the inside cooks along with the outside and remains consistently crisp.

Stem vegetables can be cooked with their skins on if they are fresh—but unless you picked them, forget it—peel them before cooking! Asparagus, broccoli and celery are good examples of stems.

Vegetables are the most abused of all the food we cook. We have been known to destroy their color and flavor through over cooking or just plain neglect. Vegetables are so often served as sodden masses of disorganized fiber with little more interest than soft, warm ice cream!

Only imagine yourself an artist with the world's garden as your palette. The colors, textures, shapes and forms before you explode with possibilities. Inhale the aroma of the whole earth and the gifts it bears.

Asparagus in Parsley Sauce
Serves 4-6

    3 tablespoons butter
    3 tablespoons flour
  ½ cup half and half cream
    1 cup chicken stock*
      Salt and freshly milled pepper
    2 egg yolks
    1 cup chopped fresh parsley
    3 pounds fresh asparagus, peeled and cooked
      crisp-tender

Prepare a roux by combining butter with flour (a paste) in a heavy skillet. Using a wire whisk, stir in the half and half and all the chicken stock. Stir constantly until thickened. Season sauce with salt and fresh pepper. Beat the egg yolks. Reduce the heat under the pan. Now add the egg yolks and keep stirring for a velvety sauce. (Remove from heat to insure **not cooking** the egg. Add the chopped parsley and let sit for 5 minutes. Re-stir to blend and serve over the hot asparagus.

Sautéed Greens Mt. Olympus
Serves 4

    3 pounds of combined: mustard, escarole,
      spinach, endive, Swiss chard
      greens—chopped into large pieces
  ½ cup olive oil
    3 cloves of garlic, peeled, crushed and minced
    2 ounces rye whiskey
      Generous pinch of dry thyme
      Generous pinch of dry oregano
      Juice of 1 fresh lemon
    4 tablespoons melted butter
      Salt and freshly milled pepper to taste

Place wet greens into a pot and steam only with the water left on the leaves until wilted and near tender. Heat olive oil in a large heavy skillet. Drain the greens well (squeeze excess water out). Sauté minced garlic until fragrant, add greens and sauté until heated through. Pour in whiskey and let steam . . . 1 minute. Sprinkle in dry herbs and stir to mix in well. Remove greens to a warm dish—dribble lemon juice and melted butter over. Season with salt and fresh pepper and serve.

Mushrooms and Artichokes

Serves 7-10

- 2 cans of artichoke bottoms (14 pieces)
  Butter for frying
- ¼ pound crab meat or shrimp—chopped
  Fresh parsley—chopped finely
- 1 303 can mushroom buttons
- ½ pound bacon—chopped finely
  Bread crumbs to bind
  Dash salt

SAUCE
- ½ cup Half & Half
- ¼ cup white wine
  Dash salt
- 1 chicken bouillon cube
- 3 tablespoons butter and 3 tablespoons flour
  (for roux)

Heat Half & Half, white wine and bouillon cube to almost boil. In a second saucepan, melt butter and blend in flour to a paste consistency (roux). Pour Half & Half mixture into roux pan and whip with a whisk. Work until lightly thickened.

In a skillet, sauté artichoke bottoms until lightly browned on edges or tender (whichever comes first). Remove to shallow oven-proof dish. Add bacon to butter and sauté until crisp. Remove and allow to cool on toweling.

In a small bowl, crumble bacon and add crab (or shrimp), chopped parsley, dash of salt and a few tablespoons of butter and bacon fat from skillet. Add bread crumbs slowly until mixture is bound.

Spoon onto artichoke bottoms and cap with mushroom. Broil for 2 minutes and serve with sauce on the side.

Poached Cauliflower and Shrimp
Serves 6

- 1 large head fresh cauliflower, leaves removed
- 1 pound medium shrimp, cooked, peeled and deveined
- 2 cups sauce cardinal*
- ¼ cup melted butter
- 1 tablespoon fresh dill weed, chopped or 1 teaspoon dry dill weed
- 1 cup fresh mushrooms, sliced
- 2 quarts water

In a heavy saucepan, poach whole cauliflower in water until tender—15 to 18 minutes. Drain and keep warm. Sauté the mushrooms and shrimp in ¼ cup of butter for 3 minutes. Add dill and sauce cardinal, and heat thoroughly. Place cauliflower on a platter and pour all but ½ cup sauce over and serve accompanied by remaining sauce on the side.

Poached Cauliflower with Cheddar Cheese and Mushroom Sauce
Serves 6

- 1 medium raw cauliflower, leaves removed
  Juice of ½ lemon
- 2 cups of sliced fresh mushrooms
- 3 tablespoons butter
- 3 tablespoons flour
- 1 cup milk or Half and Half cream, room temperature
  A good dash of freshly milled pepper
- 1½ cups shredded sharp yellow Cheddar cheese
- 1 teaspoon prepared mustard
  Salt to taste
  Chopped fresh parsley for garnish
- 2 quarts water

Place cauliflower and water in a pot large enough to hold it comfortably. Squeeze the juice of ½ lemon and simmer until crisp-tender (about 20 minutes). Drain and keep warm. Meanwhile, sauté mushrooms in butter in a heavy sauce pan for about 3 minutes. Carefully blend flour into butter, making a paste (roux). Add milk or cream all at once. Cook, stirring all the time until sauce thickens. Add cheese and cook till bubbly. Add mustard, salt and pepper. Place hot cauliflower onto a platter and pour ½ sauce over and dust with chopped parsley. Serve remaining sauce at the table.

Curried Broccoli
Serves 6-8

- 3 10 ounce packages of frozen broccoli flowerettes
- 1 8-ounce cup sour cream
- ½ teaspoon prepared dry curry powder
  A good pinch of seasoning salt
- ¼ teaspoon dry mustard
  A dash, cayenne pepper
  Salt and freshly milled pepper to taste

Cook broccoli as per package directions in a heavy saucepan, drain and keep warm.

Combine sour cream with spices and add to broccoli. Gently toss and heat over low setting until hot. Remove to vegetable dish and serve.

Summer Squash with Chicken Stuffing
Serves 4

- 2 medium zucchini or yellow summer squash— cut in half lengthwise
- 1 cup cooked chicken, chopped coarsely
- ½ cup soft bread crumbs
- 1 medium onion, minced finely
- 1 egg, lightly beaten
  Salt and freshly milled pepper
  Generous sprinkle of dry wine (dry sherry best)
- ½ teaspoon savory
- ½ cup olive oil
- 1 clove garlic, crushed and chopped finely
- ½ cup tomato sauce*
  Enough Parmesan cheese to sprinkle over all

Preheat oven to 400°. Hollow out halved squash with a melon baller (or Parisian knife) and chop coarsely.

Place ½ oil in a heated skillet and sauté onion, chicken and garlic until onion is transparent and tender . . . add seasonings and savory. Fill the summer squash hollows with this mixture. Sprinkle generously with dry sherry wine.

Pour remaining olive oil into a casserole and place filled squash securely into casserole, top with tomato sauce and a good dusting of Parmesan cheese and bake 15-20 minutes. Remove to a warm platter and serve with tomato sauce on the side.

Suggested Wine: Colli Albani—a soft fruity white wine from the hills near Rome.

Carrots and Sliced Pears

Serves 6

 1 pound fresh carrots, peeled and cross cut thin
   Water to boil carrots
 2 medium firm pears, peeled, cored and sliced
   vertical
 ½ cup mayonnaise
 3 tablespoons orange juice concentrate
   A dash of salt
 1 teaspoon toasted sesame seeds (optional)

Simmer carrots in the water covered until crisp-tender (10 minutes). Drain. Add the orange juice to the mayonnaise. Add the pear slices to the carrots and heat over very low heat. Remove when hot and toss with citrus mayonnaise. Remove to a warm vegetable dish, sprinkle with toasted sesame seeds and serve.

Yiddish Potato Knishes

Serves 6-8

1½ cups real mashed potatoes
 ⅓ cup grated onion
 2 tablespoons melted butter
   Salt and freshly milled pepper to taste
 ¾ cup sifted flour
 ½ tablespoon sugar
 ⅜ cup vegetable oil
1½ tablespoons lukewarm water
 1 egg, beaten
   Vegetable oil to grease baking pan

Combine flour, sugar and pinch of salt in a large bowl. Stir in ⅜ cup oil, water and egg to make dough. Knead for 5 minutes on a floured surface and roll out into a rectangle. Cut rectangle into thirds lengthwise and let rest. Meanwhile, in another bowl, combine potatoes, onion, butter, salt and fresh pepper and mix well. Spread ½ the potato mixture on ⅓ portion of dough—cover with the second strip of dough and spread remaining potato mixture. Finally, cover with the last dough strip. Moisten edges and press-seal. Cut into 2-inch slices with a greased, sharp knife. Place on greased baking pan—brush with oil and bake for 30 minutes or until beautifully brown at 350°. Remove to a warm platter and serve.

Florentine Artichoke Pie

Serves 4

    1 can imported artichoke hearts
      Juice from ½ lemon
    2 tablespoons olive oil
    2 tablespoons butter
      Flour
    4 eggs
      Salt and freshly milled pepper
    2 tablespoons milk

Slice the artichoke hearts as thin as possible (vertically) and spread out on toweling, pat dry if necessary. Sprinkle with the lemon juice. Heat the butter and olive oil together in a heavy skillet. Carefully dip the sliced artichoke slices into the flour to lightly coat and brown on both sides in the hot fat. Beat the eggs slightly, seasoning with the salt and fresh pepper and add the milk and mix well. Pour the egg-milk mixture into the skillet and bake in a preheated oven (350°) for 5-10 minutes, or until mixture is set. Let rest 3-5 minutes—wedge and serve on warm platter.

Asparagus with Sesame Butter

Serves 4

    12 spears of medium asparagus, cooked
    8-12 ounces fresh mushrooms, wiped and sliced
     3 tablespoons butter
     2 teaspoons sesame seeds
     1 teaspoon fresh lemon juice
       Salt and freshly milled pepper to taste

In a heavy skillet melt butter and toast sesame seeds. Add sliced mushrooms and asparagus and stir fry for only as long as it takes to heat asparagus through. Season— dribble lemon juice on vegetables and place on warm platter. Serve.

Baby Lima Beans Fines Herbs

Serves 6

    1 10-ounce package frozen baby lima beans—
      cook per package directions
    1 can artichoke hearts—drained and each heart
      quartered
    1 teaspoon lemon juice
    3 teaspoons butter
      A generous pinch each of oregano, sweet
      basil, parsley and tarragon
      Salt and freshly milled pepper to taste

Heat butter in a saucepan. Add all ingredients to butter and stir until hot. Remove to vegetable dish and serve.

Israeli Leek Cakes

Serves 4

- 1 bunch of fresh leeks (approximately 6 pieces), trimmed—wash and thoroughly rinse away sand
  Water
- 2 eggs, beaten
- 1 cup matzo meal
- 1 tablespoon olive oil
  Salt and freshly milled pepper to taste
- 3 tablespoons butter
- 3 tablespoons olive oil for frying

Simmer only the white portion of the leek in water until tender—drain and cool. Chop fairly fine and combine with egg and matzo meal, oil, salt and fresh pepper and mix very well. Allow to chill and firm. Form into patties, 3 inches in diameter and ½-inch high. Melt butter and oil in a heavy skillet and brown patties (a few at a time) on both sides. Remove to a warm platter and serve.

Scallions with Chef A's Hollandaise Sauce

Serves 4-6

- 4 or 5 bunches fresh green onions, cleaned and trimmed
- 1 cup chicken stock*
  Chef A's hollandaise sauce*
  A generous dash of nutmeg
  Orange wedges

Pour stock in a large skillet and bring to a light boil. Lay the green onions in the simmering stock and cook until barely tender (8-10 minutes). Drain and arrange on a warm platter. Add a dash of nutmeg to the hollandaise sauce and dollop over scallions. Garnish with orange wedges, making sure there's one for each person to be served.

Cucumber with Dill and Yogurt

Serves 4

- 2 large cucumbers
  Salt to taste
  Juice of ½ lemon
- 1 cup plain yogurt
- ½ teaspoon sugar
- 3 tablespoons butter
- 5 tablespoons fresh chopped dill or 3 of dry dill weed
- 1 teaspoon cornstarch

Cucumber with Dill and Yogurt
(continued)

Peel, halve and seed cucumbers, then wash under cold water, cut into bite size pieces. Place in a pan with lemon juice, sugar, salt, yogurt and 2 tablespoons butter, cover and simmer 10 minutes, stir in dill, make paste with the remaining butter and cornstarch and stir into the cucumber-yogurt mixture and cook, stirring, until thickened. Check seasonings and serve hot . . . usually in a covered vegetable dish as not to lose flavor.

Braised Fresh Celery with Dill Butter
Serves 4

    2 cups of fresh celery, bias sliced thin
    1 small green pepper, seeded and cut into
      strips
    ¼ cup water
    3 tablespoons chopped onion
    ½ teaspoon dill weed
      Salt and freshly milled pepper to taste
    3 tablespoons butter

In a saucepan place 1 tablespoon butter and sauté onions until transparent. Add remaining ingredients except 2 tablespoons butter and cover. Simmer until celery is crisp-tender (8-10 minutes). Drain. Add the 2 tablespoons butter and toss until melted. Season and serve.

Mashed Turnips with Ginger
Serves 6

    2 pounds fresh yellow turnips, pared and cubed
    1 tablespoons finely minced onion
    1 cup chicken stock*
    ½ teaspoon ground ginger (or ½ teaspoon fresh
      minced ginger)
    1 teaspoon sugar
      A dash or two soy sauce

Combine all ingredients in a saucepan, cover and simmer until the turnips are soft (maybe 15 minutes at a light boil). Drain and reserve some liquid. Mash the turnips with an old fashioned potato masher or with an electric mixer until light and fluffy, add cooking liquid as needed for moistness. Turn out onto a vegetable dish and serve.

Mushrooms in Dill Sauce
Serves 4-6

½ stick of butter
A pound of fresh mushrooms, wiped clean and sliced
Salt and freshly milled pepper to taste
1 teaspoon chopped fresh dill weed or ½ teaspoon dry dill weed
4-6 tablespoons dry white wine
½ cup heavy cream at room temperature

Melt the butter in a sauce pan and sauté the sliced mushrooms for less than a minute over high heat (stir often). Season with salt and fresh pepper, add dill weed and continue to cook short of another minute. Lower heat and add cream all at once . . . simmering, add wine slowly and reduce sauce for 3 minutes or until you're happy with its thickness. Serve over a toast crouton with extra sauce on the side.

Stuffed Cymlings
(Pattypan or Saucer Squash)
Serves 4

4 medium cymlings
3 tablespoons butter
3 green onions, chopped end to end
2 teaspoon chopped almonds
⅓ cup chicken stock*
2 tablespoons heavy cream at room temperature
Salt and freshly milled pepper to taste
½ cup freshly grated Parmesan cheese

Cook the whole squash (all 4) in boiling water for 10 minutes—drain and cool a little. Cut a ½-inch slice off blossom (that's the bumps side) and scoop out the pulp of each, leaving a quarter inch wall. Chop pulp fine. Melt 2 tablespoons butter in a heavy saucepan, add the onions and nuts and fry until well blended. Add the stock and cream and stir until thickened. Stir in chopped pulp, season with salt and fresh pepper to taste. Fill each cymling with the stuffing mixture and sprinkle with grated cheese. Place stuffed cymling squash on buttered baking dish and bake in a preheated (350°) oven for 25 minutes.

Gado-Gado

(Indonesian cold vegetable dish with sweet red pepper and shrimp sauce)
Prepare a selection of fresh vegetables:
    carrots
    parsnips
    cauliflorets
    broccoli florets
    mushrooms, sliced

Cook the vegetables except the mushrooms in simmering water until crisp-tender. Drain and cool.

SAUCE
1 sweet red pepper, stem off and seeds removed
4 ounces cooked, peeled and deveined shrimp, minced
    Pinch of salt
    Generous pinch of sugar
    Juice of 1 lemon

Heat the red pepper in hot water until soft. Pound it together with the shrimp, sugar and salt to a pulp (use blender if you like). Add the lemon juice. Arrange the cold cooked vegetables on an appropriate dish with raw mushrooms and spoon pepper-shrimp sauce over and serve.

Jewish-Armenian Moussaka

Serves 4

1 tablespoon oil
1 pound ground lean lamb
    Salt and freshly milled pepper to taste
½ teaspoon paprika
1 medium eggplant, peeled and sliced into thin rounds—(soak for 20 minutes in salted water)
⅔ cups tomato paste
½ cup dry bread crumbs

Place ground meat in a large bowl. Season to your taste with salt, fresh pepper and paprika and mix well by kneading 5 minutes. Grease an ovenproof casserole with the tablespoon of oil and press meat to line the bottom. Remove eggplant from water and pat dry and place on top of meat. Dilute tomato paste with water to almost "runny" consistency and pour over eggplant. Sprinkle with breadcrumbs. Cover tightly with foil and bake 20 minutes at 400°. Remove cover and let brown for approximately 10 minutes. Serve in casserole.

Suggested Wine: Israeli Red Wine—semi-sweet with a hint of sunshine.

Artichoke Hearts Susan Amour

Serves 4-6

 2 cans artichoke hearts, drained and quartered
 1 cup prepared mayonnaise
 ¾ cup good imported Romano cheese, grated
 ¼ cup good imported Parmesan cheese, grated
   Juice of ½ lemon
   Dash of cayenne pepper
   Paprika

Combine mayonnaise with both cheeses in a large bowl. Add lemon juice and cayenne and stir until mixed well. Add artichoke quarters and toss.

Turn into a casserole. Sprinkle with paprika and bake at 350° until slightly browned and bubbly. Serve with sesame round crackers.

Suggested Wine: White Graves—cool, dry and exciting.

Sunrise Artichoke Hors D'Oeuvre Plate

 1 medium artichoke
 ½ cup salad dressing
 1 teaspoon dry mustard
   A few dashes of Worcestershire sauce
 3 hard boiled eggs, peeled
   Salt and freshly milled pepper to taste

Cut bottom off artichoke and snip sharp points from leaves (be sure to rub the cut edge with lemon to keep from discoloring).

Cook raw artichoke covered in a large kettle of simmering salted water for about 25 minutes or until a leaf pulls off easily. Cool thoroughly; pull off all leaves. Combine salad dressing, dry mustard and Worcestershire sauce. Halve the eggs crosswise and cut each half into 8 wedges. Place a dollop of mustard dressing at the base of each artichoke leaf and place an egg wedge atop dressing on each leaf. Arrange sunburst fashion on a plate and serve. Makes about 40 leaves.

Ratatouille All'Antinore

Serves 6-8

 1 medium eggplant (1½ pounds)
 1 small zucchini (½ pound)
 1 cup green pepper, chopped and seeded
 1 large onion, peeled and chopped
 4 medium tomatoes, cut into eights
 ¼ cup olive oil
 2 cloves garlic, crushed and minced
   Salt and freshly milled pepper
 1 pound mushrooms, halved—optional
 1 stalk celery (or leaves only)—optional
 ½ pound summer squash—optional

Cut into 1-inch cubes: eggplant, zucchini, and summer squash. Lightly salt and set aside ½ an hour.

Heat oil in heavy pot. Add vegetables, in their order of cooking time: onion first, celery, garlic, eggplant, green pepper, zucchini, summer squash, tomatoes and mushrooms. Cook each addition until heated through.

When all vegetables have been added, stir and cover. Cook approximately 10 minutes, until vegetables are crisp-tender.

Serve with lots of fresh French bread.

Suggested Wine: Beaujolais, slightly chilled.

Sliced Beets and Oranges with Maple Glaze

Serves 4

 1 pound fresh beets, peeled and sliced ⅜ inch thick
   Pinch of salt and freshly milled pepper to taste
   Water to cook in
 4 tablespoons butter
 4 ⅜-inch thick orange slices
 ½ cup maple syrup

In a heavy fry pan, simmer beet slices with a pinch of salt and enough water to cover for 10 minutes, covered. Remove cover and cook until all water evaporates. Add butter, orange slices, maple syrup, salt and fresh pepper and turn over and over to coat beets and orange slices. Cook for 10-15 minutes at very low heat to glaze. Remove to appropriate dish and serve.

Pizza Carcioffi (Artichoke Pizza)

Serves 4

- 8 ounces frozen pizza dough or bread dough
- 4 ripe tomatoes or a small can of whole peeled tomatoes
- 8-ounce can of artichoke hearts
- 10 (or more) black Greek olives, pitted
- ¼ cup grated Parmesan or Romano cheese
- 1 clove fresh garlic
- 1 tablespoon freshly chopped parsley
- 3 tablespoons oil

Thaw and roll out the dough to line an 8-inch shallow pie dish. Skin and peel the tomatoes and crush onto the dough. Drain the artichoke hearts and place between the tomatoes, dot with the olives and sprinkle with the grated cheese. Crush the garlic and chop the parsley and garlic, sprinkle on the top of the tomato and artichoke mixture. Dribble with oil and place in a preheated oven (450°) for 20-25 minutes, let set for a minute or two and remove to a serving dish.

Suggested Wine: A cheerful red dry wine is in order with this delightful supper dish.

Meat and Dill Piroshki

36-40 pieces

- 1 cup (two sticks) butter
- 8 ounces cream cheese
- ¼ cup heavy cream
- 2½ cups flour
    Piroshki filling
- 1 egg
- 1 teaspoon water
- ⅛ teaspoon salt

Cream butter and cheese and beat in cream. Blend in flour and salt. Chill well. Preheat the oven to 400° and roll out dough between wax paper to ⅜-inch thickness. Cut into two- to three-inch rounds or squares. Place one teaspoon filling on one side of each round. Combine egg and water. Moisten edges of dough with mixture. Fold dough over filling, forming crescents or triangles. Seal edges. Put on a baking sheet. Brush with remaining egg mixture. Poke a small hole in the middle of each to allow steam to escape. Bake until golden, 15-20 minutes. Serve hot or cold.

Pan Bania (Pressed Sandwich Hors D'Oeuvres)
Serves 6

    1 long loaf French bread
    1 clove garlic, split
    1 cucumber, peeled and sliced
    1 tomato, thinly sliced
    3 pimientos, cut in half
    1 two-ounce can flat anchovy fillets, drained
    6 black olives (preferably Greek or Italian),
      pitted
      Olive oil
      Vinegar

Cut the bread in half lengthwise and rub the cut sides with garlic. Arrange the cucumber, tomato, pimientos, anchovies and olives over half the loaf. Sprinkle with oil and vinegar. Top with other half of the loaf and press with a heavy weight 30 minutes or longer. Remove the weight, slice into finger-size pieces and arrange on a platter and serve.

Tapénade (A Mediterranean appetizer)
Makes 2½ cups sauce

    ¼ cup capers
    3 two-ounce cans flat anchovy fillets
    1 seven-ounce can tuna fish
    1 clove garlic, or more
      Freshly ground black pepper to taste
   18 black olives (preferably Greek or Italian),
      pitted
      Juice of two lemons
    ½ cup olive oil
    3 tablespoons Cognac or brandy

Place the capers, anchovies and tuna, with the oil in which they were packed, and the garlic, olives and lemon juice in the container of an electric blender. Blend on medium speed two to five minutes, stopping the motor to stir down occasionally with a rubber spatula. Gradually add the olive oil. When all the oil is blended, the sauce should be like medium-thick mayonnaise. Blend in the Cognac and pepper. Serve at room temperature over hard-cooked eggs, cold poached fish or cold boiled beef.

Desserts 1

A perfect ending

The culmination of a meal is the dessert. By the time we reach this course we are usually far beyond the realm of what is necessary to survive, but rather looking forward to the delightful creations the cook has in store for us. Desserts are usually the treasures in a cook's repertoire; "leave 'em dazzled, and they'll rave forever!"

The art in dessert cooking, however, is in how to balance it perfectly against the courses that have preceeded. A dessert should arrive with splendor!

The realm of "perfect endings" is always an exacting science. The cook must take time to measure and follow directions with care. Beginners will be able to capture flavors and often some of the flare—but with practice, everyone can be a master at presenting dazzling, spontaneous desserts. "Keeping a good dessert table" is a right which is earned, and any cook who takes the trouble to follow the recipes, deserves the prestige.

We offer an array of easy, elegant desserts which can be prepared with little effort, producing the greatest results. They have been especially chosen because they are my particular favorites. They offer a diverse range of posssibilities adding endlessly to the media by which you create. Enjoy!

Gulab-Jamun (Indian Sweet Sponge Balls)

Makes about 20 pieces

DOUGH:
- 1 cup of non-fat dry milk
- ¼ cup flour
- ⅛ teaspoon baking soda
- 3 tablespoons melted butter (cooled)
- 3-4 tablespoons milk
- 1-1½ cups vegetable oil for deep frying

Mix dry milk, flour, baking soda and melted butter together with hands in a large bowl. Sprinkle with milk and knead until ingredients form a stiff dough. If mixture is not moist enough to knead—add a few drops of milk and continue to knead. Break off pieces of dough (about 2 teaspoons worth) and form into balls by rolling around between the palms of your hands.

SYRUP:
- 1 cup firmly packed brown sugar
- 3 cups water
- ½ teaspoon ground cardamon
- 1 teaspoon rose water

In a small saucepan, dissolve brown sugar in the water and cook uncovered for a half hour over medium heat. Remove pan from heat and allow syrup to cool.

Meanwhile, heat oil in a deep fry pan or wok and deep fry 4-5 sponge balls at a time, turning in oil to brown evenly. Remove with slotted spoon and drain on toweling.

Reheat syrup, add cardamon and mix thoroughly. Cook for 5 minutes at a simmer, add fried balls and simmer for 10-15 minutes. The balls will start to float in the syrup as they swell. When the balls have absorbed as much syrup as they can, remove from heat. Remove sweet sponge balls to a deep serving bowl. Add the rose water to the syrup and stir to mix. Pour syrup over the sponge balls and let cool 1 hour. Serve in small dessert dishes—a few Gulab-Jamun and some syrup.

Rhum Baba

Preheat oven to 375°

    1 package active dry yeast
    ½ cup warm water (105-115° F)
    3 tablespoons sugar
    2 cups all-purpose flour
    ½ teaspoon salt
    4 eggs, slightly beaten
    ½ cup raisins
    ¾ cup butter, melted
   12 ounces apricot preserves
      Juice of 1 lemon
      Rum sauce
      Sweet whipped cream

Completely dissolve yeast in warm water in a large bowl. Stir in sugar, flour, eggs, salt and raisins. Beat vigorously with a wooden spoon (or medium setting on electric hand mixer) until batter is smooth, elastic and still a little sticky. Cover with a clean towel and let rise in a warm place until double in volume (about 45 minutes).

Generously grease an 8 or 9-cup ring mold or Bundt cake pan. Stir down the batter by re-beating with wooden spoon 25 strokes. Slowly stir in butter and beat again for 5 minutes (electric mixer at medium). Pour batter evenly in mold. Cover and let rise a second time until double—45 minutes. Bake for 30 minutes at 375° or until golden brown. Remove from oven and immediately unmold—cool 10 minutes on a wire rack. Carefully place warm baba on a cake plate with a slight upturned rim. Pour about ¾ cup of the rum syrup over baba and let cool 15 minutes. Meanwhile, heat apricot preserves with lemon juice—let cool—drizzle over cool baba to glaze. Serve with a dollop of sweet whipped cream.

Rum syrup: Heat 1 cup sugar—1½ cups water—½ cup dark rum in a heavy saucepan. Stir occasionally—reduce to thicken.

German Apple Cake All'Antinore

Serves 12

4-6 small tart apples
   Juice of 2 lemons
  3 tablespoons sugar
  3 tablespoons butter, soft
  ¾ cup sugar
  2 egg yolks (separate)
   Juice of ½ lemon
  1 tablespoon lemon zest
  1 teaspoon baking powder
1½ cups flour
  ¾ cup milk
  1 tablespoon dark rum
  2 egg whites
  1 tablespoon butter (for greasing cake pan)
  1 teaspoon vegetable oil
  3 tablespoons powdered sugar

Peel apples, halve and core. Cut ½-inch deep score in each half to make fan. Sprinkle with the juice of 2 lemons and 3 tablespoons sugar—set aside.

Cream 3 tablespoons butter and ¾ cup sugar together and beat in egg yolks, one at a time. Gradually add juice of ½ lemon and lemon zest. Sift baking powder and flour together and gradually add to batter. Blend in milk and rum.

Beat the egg whites in a small bowl until stiff and fold into flour-egg-lemon batter.

Generously grease a spring-form pan. Pour in batter and place apples around the top. Brush apples with oil. Bake in 350° oven for 35-40 minutes. Remove from pan—let cool completely and dust with powdered sugar. Serve.

Peaches or Pears Alexandra

Peel fruit and boil the skins with kirsch flavored syrup (1 cup sugar, 1½ cups water, 3 ounces kirsch). Remove skins and discard. Poach fruit until firm but done. Chill cooked fruit for 2 hours in refrigerator. On an elegant serving dish, press vanilla iced-cream to ½ inch foundation. Slice fresh strawberries on the iced-cream and place fruit atop strawberries (1 per person). Dust with powdered sugar, sprinkle with red and white rose petals (rinsed under cold water to clean) and serve.

Creme Caramel

Serves 6

2 cups milk
½ vanilla bean or 1 piece of fresh lemon peel
5 eggs
½ cup sugar
3-4 tablespoons sugar for caramel

Melt the sugar for the caramel in a deep metal (smooth-sided) mold over moderate heat until it turns a deep golden brown. Remove from heat. Rotate the mold with a tilting motion until caramel coats all sides.

In a heavy saucepan, bring the milk, vanilla bean or lemon peel to a boil. Remove from heat and discard lemon or vanilla bean. Beat the eggs and sugar with hand mixer in a large bowl and pour into the hot milk a little at a time, stirring constantly. Strain the cream into the caramel mold slowly, allowing the steam to escape. Bake the contents of the mold in a pot of very hot but not boiling water over a burner or preferably, in a 375° oven for 40-50 minutes or until set. Remove the mold to a rack and cool. Unmold onto an appropriate serving platter. Refrigerate and serve cold.

Lokum (Turkish Delight)

2½ cups water
4 cups sugar
1 cup cornstarch
¾ cup orange juice
1 teaspoon cream of tartar
Whole shelled pecans or pistachios
Oil
Powdered sugar

In a heavy sauce pan, bring the water to a boil, add sugar and stir until dissolved. Combine cornstarch with orange juice and cream of tartar and mix to a smooth thick paste. Gradually pour cornstarch-orange juice mixture into boiling syrup and continue to cook for 20-30 minutes, stirring often to prevent sticking.

Oil a 7-inch square pan, 1 inch deep. Pour the hot mixture into oiled pan. Sprinkle shelled nuts into mixture and stir once around. Allow to cool. Cut into ½ by 1-inch pieces and roll in powdered sugar to coat each square.

Concord Grape and Watermelon Pie

Your favorite pie crust recipe for 2 crusts

 2 cups watermelon meat, seeds removed
3½ cups Concord grapes
 1 cup sugar
 ¼ cup flour
 ⅜ teaspoon salt
 1 teaspoon grated fresh lemon rind
 1 tablespoon grated fresh orange rind
 2 tablespoons butter

Skin the grapes and reserve the skins. Place the grape pulp and watermelon meat into a saucepan—bring to a boil and cook 2 minutes, stirring constantly. Press pulp through a sieve to remove the grape seeds. In a large bowl, combine the cooked fruit meats and grape skins. Add the flour, sugar, salt, lemon rind and orange rind and mix well. Line the bottom of a 9-inch pie pan with your favorite pastry. Fill with fruit mixture. Cover with another pastry sheet—seal and slit the top in 3 places (about 1½ inches long). Bake at 425° for 45 minutes. Cool before slicing.

Almond and Egg Cake

 2 cups toasted, crushed almonds
1½ cups sugar
 8 egg yolks
 2 tablespoons flour
 4 egg whites
 ⅛ teaspoon salt
 Lemon custard (your favorite recipe)
 Powdered sugar
 Ground cinnamon

Butter and dust with flour two 9-inch cake tins.

Combine almonds and sugar. Stir in egg yolks and flour. Beat the egg whites and salt until stiff with an electric hand mixer. Fold into egg-almond mixture. Turn equally into the cake tins. Bake at 350° for 30 to 40 minutes (watch closely the last few minutes) or until the cake shrinks from the sides of the pans. Remove from oven and cool for 15 minutes. Turn out onto platter. Spread lemon custard over bottom layer. Place second layer on top and sprinkle with powdered sugar and cinnamon. Serve a little warm.

Flemish Hazelnut Cake
1-8" Cake

     4 eggs, separated
    ¾ cup sugar
  1½ cups ground hazelnuts (any nutmeat will
       substitute)
     1 cup self-rising flour (see how easy?)
    ¾ cup powdered sugar
     1 tablespoon milk
    ½ teaspoon vanilla
    ½ cup whole hazelnuts (or nutmeats of your
       choice)

With an electric hand mixer, beat the egg
yolks with ½ cup of sugar until very thick.
Fold in the ground nutmeat and flour. Beat
the egg whites until soft peaks form, add
remaining sugar and beat until stiff. Mix ⅓ of
the egg whites into the batter until
thoroughly combined. Carefully fold in the
remaining stiff egg whites to the mixture.
The batter will be quite stiff. Turn batter into
a well buttered 8-inch spring form pan with
1½-inch sides. Bake at (preheated) 350° for
40-45 minutes or until cake tests done. Cool
5-8 minutes in the pan, then remove to a
wire cooling rack and let cool.

Mix the powdered sugar, milk and vanilla
together until smooth. Ice the top of the
cake and garnish with nutmeats.

Drowning Maidens (Germany)
Makes 4 dozen

     3 tablespoons butter
    ⅓ cup sugar
     6 eggs, separated
    ⅔ cup sifted flour
       Dash of salt
       Oil for fryer
       Powdered sugar or honey

Cream butter with electric mixer and gradually add sugar until well blended. Beat the
egg yolks until thick and smooth. Add dash
of salt and flour and make a smooth batter.
Beat the egg whites until stiff (not too dry)
and fold into the batter. In a deep heavy
skillet, heat oil to about 400°. Drop batter
into hot fat a teaspoon at a time. Turn often
to brown on all sides and cook for 2-3
minutes. Drain on toweling. To serve hot—
roll in honey to coat. To serve cool/cold—roll
in powdered sugar.

Profiteroles

For the choux pastry (cream puff pastry)

1 cup water
½ cup butter
Pinch of salt
¾ cup sifted flour
4 eggs
Filling: real whipped cream
Sauce: chocolate

In a heavy pot with a handle, bring water, butter and pinch of salt to a boil—remove from heat. Pour flour into hot liquid all at once, stirring constantly. Return to the heat, still stirring, and cook for about 5 minutes or until the mixture leaves the sides of the pan. Remove from heat again and let cool. Add the eggs—one at a time, beating vigorously after each. Beat the mixture until it becomes glossy. Spoon small dabs onto a dampened cookie sheet (walnut sized), leaving an inch or two between each. Bake profiteroles in a 400° (preheated) oven for 20 minutes (DO NOT open the oven door). Remove from oven and off cookie sheet onto a cooling rack. Prick each with a skewer to allow steam to escape. When cool, cut part way through and fill with whipped cream. Arrange on an elegant platter in a pyramid shape and refrigerate.

Chocolate Sauce:
Make basic vanilla sauce first.

1 cup milk
1 cup light cream
1 teaspoon vanilla
4 egg yolks
4 tablespoons sugar
½ teaspoon flour

Heat the milk, cream and vanilla in the top of a double boiler. Meanwhile, beat the egg yolks, sugar and flour until light and fluffy (use electric hand mixer). Pour hot milk into bowl quickly. Return mixture to double boiler and cook, stirring constantly until sauce thickens. Strain into bowl and clean double boiler.

Chocolate Sauce:
In top of double boiler, combine and melt 2 tablespoons grated Baker's chocolate, 2 tablespoons sugar in 2½ tablespoons water. When thoroughly mixed, add to vanilla sauce and blend well.

Turkish Pumpkin Dessert à la Reyhan

Serves 6

  3 pounds of fresh pumpkin
4¾ cups sugar
  ⅓ cup water

FOR THE TOPPING:
  1 cup ground walnuts

Cut pumpkin into 2½" squares and place the squares into a heavy pot. Sprinkle all the sugar over pumpkin followed by the small amount of water. Cover tightly and over medium heat allow the pumpkin to release and re-absorb it's own liquid . . . approximately 20 minutes. When cooked, the pumpkin will be tender and appear to be glossy and transparent.

Remove to a platter and garnish (sprinkle) with ground walnuts.

(Pumpkin can be cooked with the skin on and can be removed after the steaming process.)

Bettlemann
(Beggar's Pudding)

Serves 4

  ½ cup bread crumbs
  2 cups applesauce
  ¼ cup raisins
  2 tablespoons chopped almonds (walnuts good too)
  2 eggs, beaten

Combine the above, blending well. Pour into either four buttered custard cups or a buttered shallow baking dish and top with a mixture of:

  2 tablespoons each brown sugar and bread crumbs
  1 teaspoon softened butter
  ⅛ teaspoon cinnamon

Bake in 400° oven approximately 20 minutes. Can be served either warm or cold and it is especially good with a bit of cold whole milk or cream poured over the finished dish.

Index

Key:

- B = Buffet Selection
- D = Dessert
- DE = Dinner Entrée
- H = Hors d'oeuvre
- L = Lunch or Luncheon Entrée
- 1st = Appetizer or First Course

(Vegetables listed separately)